The $600 Million Dollar Latte

"There is no such thing as luck – just being in the right position."

Neil Flett

INTRODUCTION

**"Learning is so important,
it should be fun."**

This is not a business book. It's a work of fiction, but it's also filled with stuff you can use in business.

A lot of it is true, sort of. Everything in it happened, but not necessarily in this story.

Pick up some tips, while you're enjoying the story. Smile, while you learn.

Enjoy the ride, take it with a large grain of salt and if you get something that makes your life in business easier and more fruitful, then it's been a success.

Most of the names have changed, but not all. If you think I've referred to you in anything but positive terms, I unreservedly apologize… sort of.

I'd like to thank Amanda Hardwick of StudioTwoOne for the cover design, and Lesley Robinson for her endless patience and proofing.

Neil Flett

Certificate

noun

sə'tɪfɪkət/

An official document attesting a fact, in particular:
guarantee, proof, certification, document,
authorization, authentication, verification,
credentials, accreditation, testimonial, warrant,
licence, voucher, diploma

CONTENTS

CHAPTER ONE: The universal small-business challenge 1

CHAPTER TWO: There's always a way to promote yourself 19

CHAPTER THREE: Corny works everywhere! 28

CHAPTER FOUR: Go for It! 40

CHAPTER FIVE: Adding Credibility 48

CHAPTER SIX: All Hell Breaks Loose 54

CHAPTER SEVEN: The power of praise ..61

CHAPTER EIGHT: We Go National! 69

CHAPTER NINE: People Problems 81

CHAPTER TEN: We Get Some Help 88

CHAPTER ELEVEN: The Power of the Web 92

CHAPTER TWELVE: People are your business 103

CHAPTER THIRTEEN: As Simple As Can Be… 112

CHAPTER FOURTEEN: Learn From Your Past Mistakes.................................116

CHAPTER FIFTEEN: Then the World!..122

CHAPTER SIXTEEN: We've Arrived!....129

CHAPTER SEVENTEEN: Understanding the Essence...137

CHAPTER EIGHTEEN: Exponential Growth..141

CHAPTER NINETEEN: Handling Rough Times!...152

CHAPTER TWENTY: Dealing with Crises...160

CHAPTER TWENTY-ONE: Keep Smiling!..170

CHAPTER TWENTY-TWO: When you become famous...............................178

CHAPTER TWENTY-THREE: The circuit breaker...189

EPILOGUE.................................196

ABOUT THE AUTHOR...........................201

CHAPTER ONE: The universal small-business challenge

Clyde West sat in his leather recliner planning the next holiday with wife Annie. *I'm bored,* he thought as he solved yet another Sudoku, watched the news, reacted to Facebook alerts, answered his wife's chatting about hotels, thought about dinner, wondered about old workmates, sipped wine (from his own tiny vineyard) and occasionally drifted off.

I'm bored. I used to pride myself on having a worksheet of 40-50 items every day, meetings every half hour, phone calls between and during, sandwiches at the desk. Now I don't even bother to remember what day it is.

For God's Sake shut up, said Annie.

But life was not yet over for Clyde or Annie for that matter. The tedium was about to disappear because of an unheard-of little coffee lounge on a potholed road in a broken town in a faraway tropical paradise, and if he'd known that, well he would have sat up straighter.

The coffee lounge was Cassareep, on Highway 1B in Speightstown, Barbados, Caribbean - a hole-in-the wall cafe that happened to make a very good latte. And that was enough to start the whole extraordinary journey.

Before the journey was over hundreds of millions of dollars would change hands and hundreds of thousands of people would be affected. Who started it? Certainly not Iranian Sam, the owner and barista at Cassareep who could have accepted a deal of the blame because his coffee was very good. But Sam's role ceased with the serving of a single latte. Certainly not Australian Gerry Brooke who, by inviting Clyde and Annie to Barbados for a holiday, would from then on argue that he had been the catalyst for the extraordinary events that followed. Despite his endless bragging, he actually played only the smallest of parts. And certainly not any of those innocents ensnared along the way, who had no idea where one of the world's biggest money-making schemes had begun.

In hindsight, Clyde was entirely culpable, but even he didn't start out to make hundreds of millions. That just happened. Originally, he made a $15 decision to help Sam market his business a little better. He did it out of altruism, out of fun and out of a subconscious need for praise, yet it ended up generating hundreds of millions of dollars, offices in more than 190 countries and a global cult of positivity that is still going today (but not among those who always felt it a trifle unethical).

Clyde found an unbelievably simple, legal, money-making scheme that just happened to require every single marketing, PR, communication skill and business experience he'd mustered in more than 60 years. What were the odds?

It was an email from Gerry that did it.

On 08/10/2009, at 7:02, Gerry wrote:
So mate... how're things?
Martha and I will be in Barbados at Colleton House from November til March. We can't sell it until it's gone through probate so we're going to enjoy it while we can.
We'd love you to join us if you could. You'll never get the chance to experience life in a 17th century Great House on Barbados, so why not?
Love to Annie
We'd really enjoy having you here.
G.

Gerry was an old mate, a grey mountain of a man, a former rower and the personification of the word 'entrepreneur'. He and Clyde had been friends of 40 years – brothers with different mothers – young journalists together before he went into publishing boating magazines then sand mining and transport. Meanwhile, Clyde had crossed the fence from journalism into PR, management training, pitching, and communication. He'd once edited Gerry's 'Cruising Helmsman' magazine until after two years Gerry had one of his

Neil Flett

employees fire him. It was the only time in Clyde's life that he'd been dismissed and he reminded Gerry at least twice a month.

Gerry had lost his first wife to cancer and was now married to Martha and spending his time between Australia, Barbados and her home in Budapest. He'd had a life of ups and downs, with spectacular highs and terrible troughs and now it appeared his luck was changing for the better once more.

Gerry's uncle Frank had died and left him Colleton House at St Peters, near Speightstown in Barbados.

It was and still is, a historic 17th century Great House set on an extensive and picturesque seven-acre property, perched on the cliffs looking out to the Caribbean, with genuine cannon still in situ in case of pirates, despite the likelihood of an attack being somewhat diminished. One of the oldest and most distinguished properties on Barbados, it is complete with those cannon facing the approaches and probably ghosts of dead migrant (slave) sugar cane workers. It has a huge garden, with a resident gardener, wild monkeys, a housemaid and a cook.

You can Google Colleton House, Barbados (www.colletonhouse.com) If it's still for sale, the agent's blurb tells its history.

In 1647, Sir John Colleton, an English Royalist, left England and bought 90 acres of land in Barbados as his refuge. Sir John Colleton, as was the case with many Royalists at the time, suffered difficulties under Cromwell's Commonwealth though he did manage to extend his holdings to 220 acres between 1651 and 1660; He had become a sugar planter in Barbados. Colleton prospered alongside the fortunes of Barbados, which sugar made the richest place on earth.

After the hurricanes of the 18th century, very few pre-1800 buildings survived in anything like their original form; Colleton House was one of the few exceptions due to its thick walls and parapet-styled roof.

In the 1980's Colleton Great House was bought by an oil legend (that's Uncle Frank!) who immediately began renovations on the site. He initially upgraded the main house so that he could live in it while the remaining structures were worked on. The original façade of all of the buildings at Colleton was maintained, and as much of the original interiors as possible, so as to preserve the wonderful, rich history of this beautiful property and this beautiful island. The owner then transformed the old stables into his own personal museum housing some 170 tribal art pieces from Papua New Guinea. The Great

House contains tribal art, paintings, sculpture, furniture, carpets, and glasswork.

Colleton Great House remains an unbelievable home, the calibre of which is difficult to match in Barbados or elsewhere. Colleton is comprised of a grand, old five-bedroom Plantation style home made -up of two storeys and an expansive basement. Also on the grounds is a lovely two-bedroom cottage with a magnificent view of the West Coast of Barbados and out to the sparkling Caribbean Sea.

Now J.P.Morgan said that a man has two reasons for doing something: The right reason and the real reason. In this case, Clyde's right reason to visit was that Colleton House and Barbados were destinations for the Bucket List, but the real reason was to catch up with Gerry and Martha and deal with a bit of boredom.

It was a long way, but Barbados is a long way from anywhere civilized, so flying for endless hours to Bridgetown was not a deal-breaker, especially when the attraction was seeing mates and enjoying what had to be an extraordinary Great House in one of the world's playgrounds of the very, very rich.

So Annie and Clyde, in their early sixties, flew to Barbados and after what seemed like days of travel, landed in Bridgetown.

Just as it was in every brochure, Barbados was warm and sunny and grubby as they squinted their way across the tarmac to the terminal.

Gerry greeted them at baggage pick up in the airport, a calm rock amid the rush to grab bags, handle kids, and flag taxies. A bit greyer, a bit heavier, he gave Annie a huge hug then turned to shake Clyde's hand.

Didn't I fire you once?

So began the holiday in Barbados, staying at what was literally a Great House, with landscaped gardens, a tepid swimming pool and trees filled with not-so-friendly monkeys.

And that's all it should ever have been, a memorable holiday in a piece of paradise, miles from the rest of the world.

But as fate would have it, the next morning the four called into the Cassareep Café in Speightstown for nothing more than one cup of English breakfast tea, two cappuccinos, one latte and a chat.

It was, however, the start of something much bigger.

Cassareep Café had been doing an excellent job hiding itself on the beach, just off the main street in Speightstown. And Speightstown had been doing a fine job of hiding on the upper west coast of Barbados.

Barbados itself was hours from any decent world centre and although packed with English tourists from December to Easter, at other times it was much quieter, but always sunny, and around 90 degrees. Glorious mansions worth tens of millions of dollars, owned by Europeans, sat shuttered for most of the year with only the maintenance crews working in the gardens.

Speightstown itself was a small village by any standard, old, dilapidated and by no means rich, a main street beside the ocean, barely wide enough for two small cars. Shops, art galleries, a bank or two, restaurants and drinking holes lined each side of the pot-holed dusty road and everything had a sense of comfortable neglect.

The main street such as it was showed broken paving and sticky tar seal. That combination would normally have provided a local casualty ward with endless cases of sprained ankles, but because there wasn't one, it didn't.

As you walked along the footpath, keeping one eye down for trippers, you could've been forgiven for entirely missing the entrance to Cassareep. It was set between two worn buildings, six metres behind a pebbled and weedy courtyard that seemed to serve no purpose but to separate the café from the road.

No neon sign to welcome you, just an aluminum sliding door into a clean ten-by-ten room with four tables, and a coffee bar.

There was a door in the side of the building on to a very narrow stone path to the oceanfront. But there lay a scrubbed timber deck, with four more tables and a glorious view of the purest-blue Caribbean, framed by magnificent Casuarinas and white sand that together made this coast so popular, at least in the high season. This was where jet setters and locals read newspapers while sipping their coffees or eating breakfast. A hundred yards offshore, fishermen towed their nets through the tepid seas. At night Cassareep offered a Lebanese menu to locals and tourists, drawn only by word of mouth.

Gerry and Martha introduced their visitors to Sam the owner. He seemed a nice young Middle Eastern man, with his girlfriend hovering coyly just behind his right shoulder. Orders taken, the four friends walked down the side of the café to the deck to soak up the view.

When the coffee came Clyde realised two things: 1. American coffee was bad and 2. Sam's was not. The latte was rich, creamy and totally worth commenting on.

Whoa! he said between sips. *How good is this?*

It's much better than its promotion, said Gerry. *He doesn't even have a sign.*

Well, it's the best coffee I've had for weeks. American coffee is slops. This is coffee! Why isn't this place packed out? Tell him to put up that sign and promote himself.

At this point, you might require some context for that remark. Clyde used to be a reporter and feature writer, then a publicist and promoter of exhibitions, small companies and occasional corporate heavies and politicians. Promotion and publicity were second nature. He hadn't told more than a few, but he'd staged the World Bellyflop Championships at the Boat Show, an event in which eighteen-stone (minimum) men dived into a shallow above-ground pool from a three metre long springboard, landing on their fat stomachs. He who generated the biggest splash won. The event, which today would be considered a step above dwarf-tossing, gained valuable television coverage and pulled good crowds for the show - all of which goes to prove that publicity is publicity, even if it has nothing to do with the client's business.

So Clyde knew about promotion and he started to think how he would promote Cassareep if he were the owner. One of the half-truths he'd learned as a publicist of all things trivial, was that the best publicity is visual so to get exposure, you need to think about photographs and video. He'd picked that up the hard way by wasting days writing heavy, analytical media releases for the Boat Show, covering the size of the industry, the trends in boating, and the challenges facing boat retailers. Then on opening day at the show, he'd stand with his pack of releases under his arm and greet the media. To a person, the TV crews would ask: *Where's the biggest boat, the smallest, the most expensive, the cheapest, and the strangest? And if you have a girl in a bikini with a captain's hat and a bottle of champagne can you stand her on the bow of the most expensive cruiser and have her smash the bottle?*

And while it would be considered politically incorrect these days, back then he always did have those available. TV did not give a toss about the facts and figures, unless the figures were curvy.

The Bellyflop Championships worked because they were stupid, incorrect, funny, and very, very visual. He later gave the event to another publicist. Max up-staged him by running it from a wharf in the city, and benefiting from the sheer luck of having a gantry loaded with hundreds of spectators crash into the sea. Nobody died but the publicity was fantastic.

Crazy stunts created maximised publicity and Clyde and Max had been at the forefront. But there was neither time nor funding to run such an event at Cassareep. It did, however, have lots of ocean in front of it. Clyde had staged other world-class publicity events including a Bathtub

Derby in which kids drove 6hp outboard-powered bathtubs around a harbor course at break-neck speeds. It too was visual and noisy. Most of the contestants cheated like crazy by increasing the horsepower of their tiny outboards, but the Derby boasted all the elements of a good human interest story: children, speed, a bit of danger, splashes – and relevance because everyone owned a bath. It had children, speed, splashes, danger... the only element missing was animals. Still, it was wacky and visual and thus good TV - ideal for the news items screened nightly in the time slot just after the news and just before the weather. Again, though, it seemed too hard to organize it for Cassareep.

He'd promoted a $20,000 tagged fishing contest. Perhaps that could work for Sam? It would be relatively simple to run. You caught a bream the night before, tagged it and then the next morning dropped it into the Harbour as the TV cameras whirred. If anyone caught it, they'd get $20,000. The drop site would be hounded by fishermen in tin boats hoping to snag the fish seconds after it had been dropped into the sea. None did. In the following days, small craft plied the harbor hoping to hook the big dollars. Unfortunately for them (but known to the insurers) a fish caught and released was always hook-shy and probably fled to hide in fear behind a rock. Needless to say, nobody caught it, and it got the publicity. The trouble here was that any tagged fish dropped off Cassareep would probably head for Africa.

Clyde had partnered with a solo adventurer to stage a Motor Show publicity event that became one of his favorites, through its sheer creativity alone. Instead of jumping a motorcycle over thirteen double-decker buses as had been done in the past, they jumped a double-decker bus over 13 motorcycles. The crazy adventurer strapped himself into the driver's seat, wedging lifejackets between him and the steering wheel then roared across the arena, up an earth ramp and literally flew the old bus across a row of motorbikes, crashing ignominiously into the grass on the other side. A friend and media personality rode the rear platform on the bus as a conductor, right down to wearing the full uniform. Nobody was injured, a new record was established, and the client got what he needed, massive publicity on TV and front page in the newspapers. But all the buses on Barbados were still being used, as buses.

At least the jumping bus had a link to the Motor Show, unlike the April Fool's Day stunt. For weeks leading up to April 1, they ran stories in the media telling of how the same well-known personality and the solo adventurer had captured an iceberg and were towing it to the city's harbor to be cut into one-inch blocks and sold for cocktails. On the morning of April 1, people lined the Harbor and watched through the fog as the 'iceberg' floated past towed by a small motor boat which had been moored in a nearby bay until dawn, while the adventurer created his iceberg on a small barge, from rolls of white plastic draped over a wooden frame. It looked authentic and it was fun, fooling thousands, which is the only purpose of April Fool's Day. It would, however, seem odd to claim an iceberg had been found off Barbados.

But Clyde had more stupid stunts for consideration.

At the Furniture Show, he'd filled a waterbed with cheap red wine and threw roses on it. Thus the media had a '*Bed of Wine and Roses*', which made a good picture once he added the lovely girl in the sheer nightie. Today, he rued, it would not be acceptable.

Somehow a waterbed filled with wine made little sense for Cassareep, even if Sam's partner might be talked into the nightie part. What else might work?

When his client was a Chinese manufacturer of frozen dim sum Clyde had gold-plated the alleged ten-millionth dim sum and held a ceremony for the press. That, in hindsight, was probably the tackiest publicity stunt of his PR career, but it generated a lot of ink. Ends and Means.

The lesson for any small business like Sam's was simple: News needs an event, so create your own one. It doesn't have to be important, just interesting. Pictures and footage beat words every time. Clyde had had his clients turn their places of business into venues for events, ideally events relevant to the client's business, but not necessarily. When he had a publican friend who played chess for a hobby, he suggested they get the local chess master to stage a multiple-game challenge at lunchtime against any customer who could play. They had to turn up on the day with their own chess set and he would play them all at once. Minimal cost. Photos in the local newspaper and coverage by local TV. Chess?

You're probably getting the feeling that Clyde knew a lot about cheap publicity and he did. He knew how the media worked. Clyde knew, for example, that lightweight, visual, creative and **corny** stunts worked if you were dealing with certain parts of the media. He'd proven it year after year. He'd lived and breathed newspapers, edited a suburban and worked for magazines and major dailies. In between press assignments he'd worked in metropolitan radio as a journalist and newsreader, but not with any notable success. For five months in 1969, he read the radio news between midnight and 5.30am to a tiny audience of insomniacs and drunks. (Despite his constantly asking, he'd never met anybody who'd actually heard him read the radio news.) It had taken only months for Clyde to decide that he didn't like radio and it did not like him. On receiving his resignation in June, his news editor gave him a glowing reference: *Clyde West worked as a reporter from January to June 1969. He left of his own accord.* It was short and aptly summed up what had been a brief broadcasting career.

Clyde also understood promotions, contests, and events. His next job had been promotions manager of a tabloid afternoon newspaper for which he organised contests to increase the readership. Under his direction, the paper offered valuable prizes to readers for doing nothing more than filling out a coupon and mailing it. He promoted that newspaper for two years, during which the highlight was running a Win-A-Caravan contest and interviewing the winner 'live' on breakfast television. All went well until the host asked the winner where he worked, to be told he was employed by the sponsoring newspaper. They gave away two caravans in that contest.

Clyde left the paper and formed his own company with the grandiose yet humble name: Clyde West Promotions. And he stayed in PR for thirteen years, mainly as a publicist. He went on to start a successful management training company but it was the experience of those early years that piqued his interest in Cassareep's lack of marketing.

His liking of Sam, the taste of the creamy coffee, the informal ambience of the café, the stunning sand and ocean, the fact that he was on holiday, and was jet-lagged all combined to fill him with bonhomie. He was ready to help.

Gerry said he'd suggested putting up a sign, but Sam had not appeared too interested. Surely there was something more that could be done?

He needs some promotion, Clyde said. *And he doesn't have any money.*

He'd just summed up the situation faced by millions of small business owners around the world. Every dollar counted, red tape was everywhere and competition was fierce. Very few had any money to spare; all of them needed a competitive edge and even fewer knew how to get that advantage.

An hour later their coffees were finished and Sam came from behind the counter to farewell his guests. Clyde told him his coffee was excellent. *The best in Barbados.*

Thank you, said Sam, and Clyde sensed he was a tiny bit helpless. It was a look he'd seen on the faces of many of his own clients. Sam knew he was good at making coffee, doing what he loved if he could only keep going long enough to break even. The business was as broken as a Speightstown cobblestone and without money and ideas, he could do little. Sam was living the small business enigma: Desperately in need of promotion, with no money to promote.

He's a nice young guy, Clyde told Annie, as they stumbled over the broken courtyard back to the road. *He needs help.*

Yep, said Annie, *let's have a swim.*

And that should have been that.

CHAPTER TWO: There's always a way to promote yourself

But Sam's predicament was fixed in Clyde's head and the next day grew into the germ of an idea. *I've got the knowledge, skills, and experience to help Sam. In fact, if someone with my experience in PR and marketing can't help him with his publicity issues, then who can? And among those who can, who has actually been to Cassareep in Speightstown, Barbados?*

It seemed it was up to Clyde. He couldn't promote Sam's business in the traditional way because he was leaving Barbados in less than a week. Giving advice would likely be met with the blank look of somebody who'd no concept of marketing. If Clyde wrote him a plan, it would undoubtedly end up buried and unread under the paperwork. No, if something was to be done, Clyde would have to do it himself, and quickly.

He sipped a glass of Moet, watched Gerry, Martha, and Annie in the swimming pool and dwelt on the problem.

What does a business need to stand out and attract customers? It needs to be recognized. Recognition. Sam needed recognition. Cassareep deserved recognition. And what sort of recognition would draw more customers to Cassareep? What did it have that deserved to be recognized? Coffee. Coffee... Sam had to be recognized for having the best coffee on the island. OK, that's the objective, but how does a money-less businessperson get recognition, without the huge expense of advertising? They get publicity. How do they get publicity? They create a news story at their premises or they become the news story themselves.

Clyde picked up the local newspaper and scanned the pages. Sure enough, like every local paper in the world, The Speightstown Gazzette carried stories about local people, businesses, and events. None of the news was earth-shattering; in fact, most was easily-forgotten gossip and minor news. Someone's daughter won local dance fest. An attractive garden display was open for viewing. A local painter was on display in Bridgetown. A local resident had mounted a campaign to fix the potholes.

What could Sam do to get publicity for his coffee? The usual way would be to take advertisements and boast about his coffee. But he had no money. He couldn't sponsor anything because that also took money. He couldn't give a donation to charity. He wasn't the sort to speak out on behalf of other business people. He wasn't a sportsman, not even a member of Rotary, if it even existed in Speightstown.

But he did make an exceptional coffee. Could that gain recognition?

Perhaps. Clyde cast his mind back to the lengths he'd gone to in promoting furniture shows, motor shows, and boat shows. And a germ of an idea began to grow. He drained his Moet and called out to Gerry: *I'm borrowing the car. Back in half an hour.*

As he drove down from the hill into the town, he decided he could do it with a promotional budget of no more than $15, *(*a lot less than he'd normally charge, but he was retired and on holiday*)*. In the local general store, he purchased a picture frame, simple black plastic around plain glass, the size of an A4 letter. Then he drove back to Colleton, getting more and more excited as he approached the huge gates. He asked Gerry if he could borrow the computer and Gerry dried himself off and followed upstairs.

Clyde tapped away at the Apple Mac and made something for Sam. It was a certificate. On 'official' International Coffee Drinkers Society letterhead, pilfered from Microsoft art. He explained what he was doing and Gerry suggested he change the name to *"International Society of Coffee Connoisseurs",* because it sounded more 'wanky', as he put it.

After five minutes it looked like this:

The award was for three years because, as they agreed, small businesses benefit from delivering quality product over time. He was sure Cassareep's coffee was no flash-in-the-pan.

But credibility was needed too. With only the smallest of ceremonies, he made Gerry the

Chairman of the Society and took the CEO role for himself.

My magnanimous act in appointing you Chairman shows that I bear no grudges despite your having had one of your minions fire me as editor of your crappy boating magazine.

Gerry replied that it had only been crappy because of Clyde's efforts.

They each signed the bottom of the certificate with a flourish.

That'll do!

Clyde slotted the newly-printed certificate into the frame, put in the cardboard backing and bent over the metal prongs.

You can smell the credibility, Gerry said.

Too right, said Clyde. *We're the founding members of the International Society of Coffee Connoisseurs. We're international travellers who love our coffee and we travel the world and recognize great brews. That's credibility!*

Time for a Moet.

You can't argue with that, said Gerry shaking Clyde's hand.

And thus the first hurdle was overcome. In their own minds, they'd informally created a Society dedicated to good coffee and had done so with a handshake. Who knew then how many more ethical barriers would be swept aside in the years to come.

They visited Cassareep the next morning and held a small, informal (*yet powerful and moving,* thought Clyde) presentation ceremony. Sam came out from behind his coffee machine and Clyde asked him to stand next to Gerry. He was curious but politely waited while Clyde opened the crinkled brown paper bag and made a short, poignant speech:

Sam, as CEO and founder of the International Society of Coffee Connoisseurs, I am delighted to announce that your barista skills have been recognized internationally. I hereby award you the certificate for best coffee in the Caribbean, 2007-2009. Congratulations!

Sam gulped, turned the certificate around, read the front, looked confused then gave a tentative smile.

Gerry somewhat spoiled the moment by adding: *We didn't do this for free coffee, of course.*

Next followed a quick check of Cassareep's internal walls and a decision to hang the certificate between two photographs of the beach. Sam hammered in a tiny nail and hoisted the certificate on to it. And there it sat proclaiming to all that Cassareep was better - no not better, the BEST – place for coffee in the Caribbean.

They left Sam and his staff member staring at the wall, wondering what had just happened. Clyde and Annie laughed their way to the car, mission accomplished. Back at Colleton House they sat on the patio, watched the monkeys run through the trees around the yard and drank champagne.

That's was a really nice thing to do, Annie said. *He deserves it.*

And Clyde felt that he'd done just a little to make Sam's life better.

Just to make sure it wasn't a totally meaningless exercise, Clyde rang the local paper anonymously and spoke to the editor.

Four days later, they again drove down to the Speightstown cove for a 29-degree swim and then next door for a Cassareep coffee. The certificate had generated comment. The little piece of paper had people talking, first customers, then the local newspaper reporter. She'd published an article on Cassareep, with a lovely photo of Sam and his staff member posing in front of the certificate.

When she'd asked Sam about the certificate and the Society, he'd shrugged and told the truth: *Two guys came in and presented it to me. They loved my coffee. You should try one, on the house.*

She accepted and wrote a beautiful human-interest piece.

Ah, it's good to know that journalists are the same the world over, thought Clyde. *You're more likely to get positive coverage if they like you. And a free coffee helps.*

He was right. The times of truly investigative reporting were, in the main, done and dusted. The average age of suburban news reporters was the early twenties and on any day a reporter might cover four or five different news events, so they never got the chance to learn much about any story - at least until they specialized in one area. If the story was relatively lightweight, then they usually wouldn't bother to dig too deeply… in this case, checking to see if such a society had even existed.

The Cassareep award was just another filler for the paper. The article and photograph were published in a newspaper that the next day wrapped fish. The editor was happy. Sam was happy. And Clyde was happy too.

But the effect on Sam's business was significant. Within days he noticed trade had started to pick up. He cut out the article and framed it to hang on the wall beside the certificate, where both became points of interest for customers. And as always happens, those customers mentioned it to their friends, who also visited, and told friends.

With one simple act, Cassareep had been lifted above other Barbados cafes. It was, in a word, special. It had been given recognition by an unbiased, credible, third party. Worth having!

Meanwhile, Clyde and Annie had flown home.

CHAPTER THREE: Corny works everywhere!

When Clyde was a young journalist, a fellow cadet drove a bright red Alfa Romeo sports car. Clyde, on the same salary, had one scruffy suit and drove a Morris Minor 850. Alastair wore smarter clothes and drank only imported beers. Clyde thought he must be from wealth, but his family wasn't rich. The salary of a cadet was 7 pounds per week (and 8 pounds fifty pence if the cadet could do 120 words per minute in Pitmans shorthand.) Even having achieved the shorthand target in three weeks and forgotten all but two symbols a week later, Clyde still drove his clapped-out, poo-brown Morris Minor, not a sparkling red chick-magnet.

Then one night over a few beers, Alistair told Clyde how he made serious money on the side.

I run this ad in the back of People magazine, he explained. *It says: 'To find out how to make thousands of dollars, simply send two pounds with a stamped, addressed, envelope to this PO Box.'*

I make thousands of pounds a year, he boasted.

Clyde was stunned. *What do they get for their money?*

I send them a piece of paper advising them to run an ad in People magazine telling readers they should send two pounds to find out how to make thousands.

Evidently, people did.

That seemed a brilliant, harmless concept to Clyde, a broke nineteen-year-old cadet reporter. Certainly, nobody suffered and each reader who responded was living proof that the moneymaking idea in the advertisement really worked. But for some reason, a few months later the spoilsport publisher of People stopped accepting the advertisements.

What stayed with Clyde was the appeal of 'a lot for a little.' It seemed that people responded if they could see a large benefit for a little-or-nothing outlay. Some people couldn't stop themselves investigating the *too good to be true.* Clyde didn't try Alistair's scheme himself but he never forgot "a lot for a little." If customers only have to pay a little for a lot of benefits, then the number of customers will grow exponentially.

The choice in business, he'd decided, was that you either had to have a few customers each delivering a huge margin or a huge number of customers each paying you a small margin. Mediocrity lay between the two.

Back home in the bungalow in his beachside suburb, Clyde was thinking occasionally of Sam and of Cassareep.

He'd retired from his training company and didn't want or need work. He'd run companies since he was 24 and was well and truly over hiring and firing people. He wanted to travel and relax, perhaps write, or perhaps not.

But he did enjoy a good latte and in his quest for one with a creamy texture and rich, deep taste, (with that little drawing of a tree in the cream) he went with his son-in-law to a friend's cafe on the beach.

It's one of the Campos chain, said Phil, as if that meant something. *They send mystery shoppers around to make sure the quality is the best and if it isn't, they lose their license.*

Wow, that means they must be good, thought Clyde cynically.

The coffee was excellent and as he sipped, Clyde thought back to Cassareep. Unlike that romantic coffee house, this beachside cafe seemed busy and had the usual local art for sale on its walls (why pay for decoration when you can get a cut for selling someone else's crap art?). But Clyde realized he'd found in the owners yet another case of a couple with aspirations who had taken a risk to begin a new life, only to find it was really hard to build a profitable trade.

Terry and Lisa only made money if they were packed out and when they were, they were caught in another small-business conundrum: When it boomed they needed more people, but they weren't always busy. If they hired staff, they had to carry the extra overheads through the slow patches.

Clyde decided they were struggling as a business and felt obliged to help. What's more, he had the means to do so.

The next morning, the International Society of Coffee Connoisseurs issued its second award. It nominated 'Bella's By The Sea' as being the best coffee on the Peninsula. This time the frame cost $14, but what the hell.

Clyde realized that having real names as signatories on the certificate did nothing for credibility, so he took his name and Gerry's off the bottom. Instead, he scrawled an impossible-to-read signature above the title of CEO and Chairman. He printed the certificate on semi-gloss paper and fitted it in the cheap frame.

Next morning Annie and Clyde ran another moving ceremony in the coffee lounge and it went well, but with a minor problem, in that, while Terry accepted the award, he was suspicious from the start.

What is this? he said. *Why are you giving it?*

Clyde said *I find the best coffee for the Society. I nominated you.* All of which was true.

Just shut up and take it, said Lisa. *It's free.*

And again, that should have been that. But unlike Sam in Barbados, Terry was a persistently curious soul. He went online to find the Society and of course, found nothing. He could have left well enough alone – *after all*, thought Clyde, *HE didn't pay $14 bucks for a certificate. I did.*

When Clyde next called in for a latte, he found himself confronted. *There's no such society!* Terry said righteously.

Where's the trust? thought Clyde, red-faced and not wanting to be exposed in front of his relatives.

Instantly he blurted: *The site's under construction. It'll be finished by Friday.*

That's not really a lie, thought Clyde. *It's just a timing issue. It wouldn't be a lie if he asked me next Saturday.*

The ability to tap dance his way out of tough spots came partly from childhood growing up as the youngest in a family, and often being accused of doing things like turning his sister into an ornithophobic by locking her in a chicken coop and going off to visit a mate. Clyde was good at tap dancing. It's what he'd done as a freckle-faced youngster and continued to do as a publicity person dealing with clients' unreasonable expectations. Some might call it telling fibs. Clyde liked to think of it as 'Truth well told.'

He rushed home, grabbed the phone and rang an IT friend. Nigel had been an employee and a mate for years. As CEO, Clyde would constantly wreak havoc with his computer, impatiently pressing buttons too quickly, uploading virus-filled programs, deleting work… and Nigel had calmly seen him through it all. Even if he happened to be 10,000 kilometres away in the London or New York offices, he'd log on to Clyde's screen and take over his computer, eerily fixing everything before signing off.

Now he lived in New Zealand and was happy to help.

Do it yourself, he said. *Any idiot can do it. Even you. Go online to Crazy Domains.* So Clyde did.

It cost him just $76.00 and he owned a domain name:

www.ISOCC.com.au

For another $299 he bought a kit on How To Make Your Own Website. So he did that too. As

Nigel had said, he was the perfect confirmation that any idiot could do it.

The newly-crafted ISOCC web page had a main page displaying a draft certificate and a few words describing the ISOCC's love of coffee and its determination to reward the best baristas in the world. There was a photograph (from clip art) of two people drinking coffee and a Contact link that enabled readers to send an email to Coffee@ISOCC.com.au

Suddenly ISOCC existed! Clyde emailed himself to check it was working. It did seem a deal of trouble and expense for just two certificates, but faced with the prospect of more embarrassing coffees, it was worth it. With a few dollars, he'd bought himself credibility. *The web*, he thought, *is about lots of information, not quality.*

Yet again, Clyde was right. Unlike the tactile mainstream press which you can hold in your hands, on-line images are on-screen only fleetingly. But anything that carried the written word added credibility.

Coffee-shop owner Terry looked it up and was placated, which goes to prove that if you really want to believe something it doesn't take much to convince you.

Meanwhile, fate was playing its hand again. Somebody had told a cadet journalist from the local newspaper about Bella's having a certificate from an international coffee society. The tipoff was a phone call from a woman who called herself Amelia because Annie preferred not to be recognised. A young reporter wrote a personality piece about a young couple that'd taken a risk by opening their own coffee lounge, only to find themselves awarded international recognition. Terry proudly pointed her to the website, because it was evidence that the certificate was real. And in the paper three days later there was the photograph of the happy couple holding Clyde's certificate.

In what Clyde considered to be a major plus, the reporter had even gone online to check the credentials of the ISOCC and had confirmed certificates had been awarded in Barbados and now Bella's. And she quoted the ISOCC CEO: *The ISOCC is a Society dedicated to fine coffee.*

Clyde had used two skills from his past, two skills that any small business could use: He'd created a news event and made sure it was reported in a local newspaper. And, as always, it had worked.

To celebrate he logged on to Trip Advisor and gave Bella's By The Sea a solid recommendation. Annie did the same. *Our experience was wonderful,* she gushed. *The owners are beautiful people and the coffee is simply the best. It is a part of the Campos chain and they send mystery shoppers out to check the baristas are only making the best coffee. I'd recommend Bella's to anybody.*

Despite some media claims, there's nothing to stop anyone promoting their own business on travel websites. The web is basically anonymous. And the written word and end-user testimonials make powerful evidence.

So that is that, Clyde thought. *I've helped someone else out and it feels good.*

He poured himself a glass of wine and drank it with his feet up on his study desk. There was a ping on his commuter screen. He checked the ISOCC email account and found four emails, all from coffee lounge-owners asking for the ISOCC to try their coffee and asking how they might get a certificate. He poured another glass. *Amazing,* thought Clyde, *Two of them have asked how much it would cost... What's happening here? Four emails from one story in a suburban newspaper. It's bizarre. Is it something about coffee?*

Without any effort at all, Clyde had four potential customers - four more small businesses, he told himself, who obviously needed his help.

I should, he told Annie.

Should what?

Do four more and send them off with press releases. They need me.

Are you barking mad, she replied. *It's costing us money and time. What's in it for you?*

And she added some unprintable stuff and stormed off.

She's right, he said to himself. *The last thing I need is to go to the mall, look for a parking space, buy frames, wrap, create media releases, go to the post office. She's right. I'll just fulfill these obligations by doing four more. She's right.*

He topped up his glass. He remembered standing in a tiny café in a country town and reading a press clipping pinned to the wall. It was a story and photograph of the owner and his small, fat American Staffordshire dog. It told how the barista had donated half of one day's profits to help the St Vincent de Paul Society. Half of one day's profits, probably about $100.00. And in return, he'd had a story in the local paper with a photograph of him and his dog, whose contribution seemed to be sleeping on the floor or in the doorway and farting endlessly.

Good on the café owner for supporting charity and gaining the benefit of publicity. An advertisement would have cost him $1,000 and it would not have been as well read. When

Clyde ran publicity companies, he'd created a magic formula that told clients that one story was worth six times the value of a similar-sized advertisement. That was because, he'd told them, people buy newspapers (or unwrap the free ones tossed over the fence) to read the stories, not read the advertisements. *The ads are placed around the stories in hopes that the readers' eyes might stray,* he'd say with authority. Well, that's what he said as a publicist. The advertising representatives had their own version.

That night Annie and Clyde had drinks on the terrace, he a glass of their own tiny vineyard's The Hunter Vineyard 2010 Traminer **(www.thehuntervineyard.com.au)** and she, a Peroni beer. Clyde told her he was going to send off four more certificates.

It's a waste of time, she said.

Well, I've got plenty of that,

Why would you bother? You don't need work.

*Perhaps I do. Driving you to the supermarket and pushing the trolley around behind you is not exactly challenging. (*No bitterness there.)

But the whole thing is shonky she noted, hitting a well-exposed nerve.

No, it's not! We have a sort of real society. We happen to issue certificates. Who says we can't issue more. It's not illegal. I think there's a market for recognition among those who can't afford to generate their own. Anyway, we can always give them their money back if it blows up.

What! You're going to charge them! Are you mad? You'll end up in jail! It's fraud!

It is not. It's sort of legit.

Well, leave me out of it! she fumed, reaching for her glass.

Subject closed.

CHAPTER FOUR: Go for It!

In life we make decisions based on our guiding values, Clyde reminded himself. It was what he'd taught eager business executives for years in workshops.

We have Experience Values, he'd say, which *come from everything we've done in our lives, good and bad. They are the life lessons that affect how we make decisions today.*

For example: I won't buy a used car from a dealer because I was ripped off once; I won't smoke cigars again because the last time I did, I vomited for hours; I won't give my bank details out over the phone, again...

Then we have Current Imposed Values that also affect how we make decisions e.g. I don't have enough money. My partner won't let me. I don't have a license. The market is down right now. I need insurance desperately. My partner won't let me. (So common I mention it twice.)

Our Experience and Current Imposed Values guide us in decision making.

I'm sick of being retired, he thought. *That's a current imposed value and I've fallen for it. What if I can use my experience values? What if I use values from every job I've ever had?*

And what if I took risks like Gerry does?

Gerry was probably the most brilliant and courageous opportunist you could ever meet. Pragmatic on the one hand and intuitive on the other, Gerry had been contemplating bankruptcy when he walked across a paddock on his 100-acre farm and noticed the quality of the sand underfoot. It was particularly fine and he sent it away to be assayed. (How many people would ever think to do that?). Sure enough, it was of the quality used on golf course greens. He made a few calls and hired an excavator. Then he rang around the local mining truckies and asked if they wanted work for their trucks in their spare time. He sold sand to golf courses, had it carted in the trucks of his newly-found mates and turned a barren paddock into a multi-million-dollar sand mine, at least until the neighbours and the Council closed him down because up to 100 trucks a day rumbled past their front doors. He sold that farm and bought another on the river away from neighbours and kept mining sand. And he learned about trucking.

Gerry took his new-found knowledge and approached the contractors cutting a tunnel under the city. He negotiated to help them cart away their sandstone waste. Then he rang another contractor building a major ring road and asked him where they were buying their rock fill. Then he called his truckies again and he was back in business being paid to cart stone away and being paid to deliver it somewhere else.

Clyde had always admired the way his friend could find opportunity where nobody else could. He'd created openings that nobody else could imagine. Not all worked but some did, with spectacular results.

That's what's needed here, he said into his glass.

This certificate business was bizarre and on a tiny scale. It probably would just fizzle out, but something was happening and Clyde couldn't put his finger on it.

What if Annie wasn't right? he mused. What if I made just a few bucks, so I covered the overheads? Travel money, a few meals out. Nobody's hurt if a certificate costs very little and gives a big return. I've got nothing else important to do. If I can help a small business gain local publicity for a few dollars, that's something that's almost philanthropic!

What was there to lose? This new business - if it ever evolved beyond four more certificates - carried no downside that Clyde could think of. Time to test the waters.

He wrote back to each of the four emailers and explained that if they put their cafe names forward, the Society would consider them for a certificate, the cost of which was $114.00. He was careful to leave the impression that there might or might not be a visit and tasting in a sort of 'mystery shopper' manner, but he didn't actually state that. Instead, Clyde wrote: *The ISOCC has a selection process by which it finds award-winners. In the case of your business, that process has now started.*

Then he thought some more and made it: *$144, including certificate and an elegant black frame.'*

That price, he told himself, *equates to $2.76 a week for a year – not an impost on any business.*

But there were logistics to also consider. How to get paid? He could ask for cheques, but who did that anymore? Cash would ring alarm bells. Reluctantly, he gave them his personal bank account details so they could transfer the money.

He was stunned to find a week later, his account had an extra $288 in it. Clyde filled out and printed two more certificates, personalizing them for each café and then he went a bit further, writing and tailoring a one-page press release to suit each suburb and adding some instructions for the certificate winners.

I'm just nipping down to the mall. Won't be long, he called out to Annie and he went out and bought frames, bubble wrap, envelopes, and stamps at a cost of $28 and mailing of $9.70.

A day later another $288 arrived. *I'm just going down to the newsagency,* he called out as he went back to buy frames, envelopes, and mail.

It had taken a bit of time, but he'd covered the cost of the website and mailing and a couple of lattes.

It wasn't just the certificates, he told himself. *None of the requests would have happened without that story in the local newspaper.* When he sent out the ISOCC certificates, he'd included the media story for the recipients to forward to their local newspapers and community magazines. He suggested his new members telephone and tell the editors of their success. (If they didn't, Ms. Anonymous would anyway). He'd learned years ago that local newspapers preferred to deal directly with the people who made the news or with local tipsters, not with public relations companies. *If you genuinely think you have a story*, he'd tell clients, *ring up and say this...*

But publicity was also very fleeting, so in his email to each recipient, he suggested that they frame any press clippings from the local newspapers and hang them on the wall. Some former clients had received local coverage but then did nothing. The next day their story was literally wrapped around fast food, but if they had framed it and put it on the cafe wall, it lasted for years. *When you're small and budget-less,* preached Clyde, that *extended publicity is gold.*

After years of working with suburban newspapers and not really caring about them, Clyde had finally understood their importance in the local community. As a publicist, he'd considered them a source of clippings that he could show his clients, but from the paradigm of the small businessperson they'd become much more powerful because the suburban paper's readership was made up of those who shopped and dealt with local businesses. This vital media tapped into communities, whose members supported it, lived off it and contributed to it.

Clyde should have known that from his past. When he promoted the Boat Show he created the Miss Boat Show Quest and raised money for the Autistic Children's Association, a cause well worth supporting. To promote the Quest and the Show he had attractive entrants photographed in swimsuits next to a boat on a beach, wearing their beauty pageant sashes e.g. Miss Mercury Outboards, Miss Top-rate Tackle (his personal favorite) or Miss Enterprise Marine. Then, to gain publicity, he sent those photographs to every suburban newspaper in the city, with a story about their local entrant in the Miss Boat Show Quest, because local papers like to celebrate local people and ONLY local people. If the girl was from a different suburb, forget it!

But the show required coverage in too many newspapers and there were only eight girl entrants most of them friends and relatives, so given the fact that the end was more important than the means, Clyde had the same eight girls pose for 40 sponsors. Even Annie threw on a sash and helped out (Miss St George Motor Boat Club). They photographed each girl 5 times and just changed sashes. Who says PR people aren't creative?

The publicity was exceptional. Busy journalists on local newspapers took the photos and stories and ran them. Everybody won. The quest raised $2,477.00 for the Autistic Children's Society, the Boat Show got publicity and the local newspapers each had a free story. Nobody asked why their entrant had never been heard of locally. Clyde was still surprised that no sponsors ever saw their girls also wearing another sponsor's sash. But no one felt any pain. And that's the point, he'd decided, a little bit of exaggeration is fine, as long as nobody suffers.

Local newspapers run stories about locals. Any stories. And most young journalists are overworked and/or a little bit lazy. Clyde could say that because he had been one. It meant they didn't always delve into backgrounds and often took someone's word at face value.

And now, of course, there was no subterfuge anyway. The ISOCC had a website, so the reporters could easily check it out.

As he had found in Barbados, suburban newspapers tended to be training grounds for young reporters, inexperienced, too busy, and sometimes too trusting.

Writing the ISOCC press release was not a chore. Clyde wrote one master and modified it for each winner. Each was the same but for a couple of minor changes. It consisted of an announcement that a certain coffee lounge in the newspaper's circulation area had been recognized with an international award. Clyde just inserted a new name and address each time depending on the specific lounge.

Within two weeks, four more stories ran in four different community newspapers.

And he had another four orders for certificates. $576 before costs.

CHAPTER FIVE: Adding Credibility

But Clyde was feeling guilty about his own credibility or lack thereof. There was no actual 'International Society of Coffee Connoisseurs' beyond the cheapest of websites and the 'Society' did not have a bank account as such, or members, or anything except Clyde.

He rang his lawyer and asked him how much it might cost to form a real Association called The International Society of Coffee Connoisseurs. It turned out to be very simple and very cost-effective. And online.

The Department of Fair Trading needed five members of like-interest to sign up, so he invited his wife Annie, daughters Kirsty and Melinda, their husbands Brent and Phil, to join the Society, as lovers of fine coffee. Annie pointed out that she hadn't drunk coffee for 30 years, but Clyde told her it would be politically incorrect to ban her just because she only drank tea. He did not want to be sued.

The Society members' payoff was to be the Annual General Meeting which Clyde promised would occur at the Aria Restaurant. And membership was of course free. It's amazing how simple it is to form a Society. Clyde

Googled and found software to manage association membership. How easy was that! He decided to even let Annie run it. *Get stuffed,* she said enthusiastically.

The second credibility issue was the use of Clyde's personal savings bank account. It drew attention to the reality that there was a single person behind the Society. Clyde needed the Society to have its own account and that turned out to be just as easy.

He visited his local bank branch and met Ivan. For a bank manager, he looked too young, about 12 and a bit spotty, but he was as keen as mustard to open new accounts. Clyde showed him his passport, driver's licence and a copy of his Society's framed (simple black frame $14) Certificate of Incorporation and Ivan showed Clyde how to open another bank account in the name of the ISOCC.

How many members does your Association have? he asked.

A small number, but rapidly expanding, Clyde replied.

Do you think your members might be interested in banking with us? Ivan asked nervously.

I'll ask them, said Clyde. *Perhaps you might advertise for customers on our website?*

I don't have a budget, but I could ask Head Office.

Sure.

Neither had any intention of following through.

Now not only did Clyde have a legitimate Society with members, a website, with the potential for advertising, but he also had a bank account called ISOCC.

Back home he added the new account details to the website and made a note to include them in all future emails. He also created an onsite blog and asked the question: *'Is organic coffee really better?'* A Society member added to the blog. *'MS of Newport'* argued strongly that organic coffee was NOT better. Clyde was proud of her, especially because Annie only drank tea and beer.

Two days later he had another $288 in the account and printed off two more certificates. That night Clyde poured a glass or two of 2011 Hunter Vineyard Gewurztraminer, and started to imagine… Where could this radical concept go?

By bottle end, it was becoming exciting.

If he issued 10 certificates? $1440. That would almost cover the cost of the Annual General Meeting.

What if it was 100? $14,400.

1000? $144,000.

10,000? $1.4million!

He opened another bottle, this time the 2012 The Hunter Vineyard Reserve Press Gewurztraminer.

100,000? $14.4million!

Dreaming is a legitimate and essential part of the life of a small businessperson. Without dreams, you can't stay motivated. The bigger the dream, the harder you work.

He didn't need the job, but this bizarre goal was simply worthy of pursuit. And a bit hilarious! Perhaps there was life beyond completing the diabolical-level Sudoku each day. Perhaps retired people didn't **all** do cryptic crossword puzzles.

And there was also a little altruism involved. He'd been a small business owner. He'd lain awake at night worrying about the overdraft. One year he'd actually purchased seven Christmas Club accounts from his bank manager (who was on a drive to sell them) in hopes he would not call in Clyde's overdraft. The manager didn't and the business survived.

So if Clyde could help small coffee lounge owners by getting them some good publicity for very little, why not? As long as the value delivered was more than the costs incurred, Clyde could live with himself.

With the help of Mr. Gewurz, Clyde decided to push it just a little further.

When he'd run his publicity company, he used to make a presentation to potential clients, educating them about PR. As a creative opening, he'd hold up two copies of the same daily newspaper. The first would be a complete edition. Then he'd display another copy of the paper, with every story that had been placed with the help of a public relations person, scissored from it. He included political media liaison people (which decimated the entire politics section), all public relations people working for retailers, manufacturers and distributors, (which killed off the features and homeware sections,) then added sports managers and promoters and police media people, (which virtually destroyed anything left of the paper.) What remained were display advertisements, general news reports on disasters, shipping columns, classifieds and weather reports.

His point was that the news media, mainly through cost-cutting, has been left in a state in which it relied overwhelmingly on leads and stories from publicity people, media managers, Government minders and corporate affairs directors. It was the only means available to fill its pages without paying for hundreds of extra journalists on staff.

Today, in fact, the larger corporations actually write tailored releases for particular journalists in different media, and the busy journalists often just run them.

So he'd become an expert over the years in how to generate stories, helping publishers cut their costs by having PR people do the work of the journalist. He'd publicized Rolls Royce for years and the national financial newspaper ran his new-model announcement unchanged, except for adding the by-line of their motoring writer. Clyde took it as a compliment.

His new business model was taking a unique shape. It used the emotional desire of its clients to be recognized with a certificate from an international society PLUS the newsworthiness of those very small businesses having gained that recognition PLUS the need of suburban newspapers to find stories about businesses in their area. Everybody was a winner!

But the ISOCC small business was very small and growing too slowly. Community media only covered one or two suburbs at a time, so getting the ISOCC word out could take a long, long time. Being 63, Clyde did occasionally consider how much effective time he had left. It was time to take a gamble.

CHAPTER SIX: All Hell Breaks Loose

Luckily, doing the journalists' work for them was not a strategy limited to community newspapers and magazines. The national newspaper went to every part of the country with a circulation of 250,186. Clyde wrote a story/release about the international acclaim that the local coffee lounges were receiving. He sent it to one of his journalist contacts who passed it on to a colleague. With few changes it ran nationally under the heading: *'Our Coffee takes the world by storm.'* One of Clyde's certificate recipients had a photograph included, holding the certificate.

Clyde had Nigel create a drop-down menu for the website with *'Media Mentions'* section and placed all the articles in it, including the national coverage. How deliciously ironic. He was the organiser of the stories and was now using them as an unbiased third-party endorsement of his own business.

All hell broke loose.

Whether it was the trendiness of barista coffee or the love of certificates generally or the desperation of small business, the ISOCC website received 59 enquiries and 38 orders

($5,472) within a week, from coffee lounges all over the country. Plus, there was a radio interview with one delighted café owner.

Why do you think the Society chose you? the DJ asked.

We go to a lot of trouble to choose the right beans and our barista is fully-trained, said the owner.

Well done, said the DJ. *I hope everyone drops in to try it. I'm certainly going to!*

What had that free plug been worth to the café owner? Who knows, but it would cost thousands to buy an advertisement to say the same. The ISOCC had achieved it for $144.00, including the certificate and the newspaper article now framed on the wall beside it.

There is an aura about coffee, thought Clyde. *Everyone has their favorite coffee shop. Everyone likes to be seen drinking a well-known brand.* He knew the whole barista persona had become chic, but perhaps he'd misread just how cool it had become.

First things first. He went to Cosco and priced 200 frames. $2,800. That wouldn't work. He bought 38 instead, printed off the certificates and framed them, carried them down to the Post Office, put them in padded envelopes and mailed them, along with draft releases for their local newspapers. Annie and Clyde went on to Trip Advisor and gave them each a good wrap.

But it took all day!

You might think that by now Clyde should have been feeling ethically challenged, but he'd counter that thought with the convincing argument that he was doing harmless good for people who did not have the funds to market themselves. He was a virtual PR company to companies so small they could not afford to pay more than $144 for publicity. No publicity company would ever generate such coverage for $144, so he was being very generous. And the most important check was to ask: *If the recipients knew how small the Society was, would they give back their award?"* Clyde doubted it.

But quality assurance was lacking. Make that non-existent. What if a member's coffee was horrible, filled with grit, tasteless and thin? *Well*, he told himself, *in a competitive market like today, they wouldn't be in business, except in the USA where they would excel. The fact that they were surviving meant their coffee had to be worth having.*

Clyde's job was not to make the coffee, but to promote it. That's a train of thought that some PR people cling to all their lives. *My job is not to make cigarettes, but to promote them. My job is not to make liquor, but to promote it.*

Clyde thought about vineyards, many of which produced poor wine, but whose owners wrote glowingly of it on their websites. He remembered vineyard owners in a region close to a major city who when they failed to win medals in the major shows, started their own local show, judged their wine themselves, and marvelously won medals.

Who doesn't exaggerate out of pride and commercial need? In fact, dear friends of Clyde's had written a testimonial for his Gewurztraminer by stringing together words from the backs of other people's wine bottles. It read well:

The Hunter Vineyard 2009 Traminer carries front-of-palate flavors of elderberry, ginger, licorice, and mint with hints of blackcurrant.

Exaggeration in business is legitimate, he told himself. *Every business small and large does it every day, led largely by real estate agents. It's how small businesses get bigger.*

Clyde had been trained in how to do it by years in PR. You'd claim to be something then you'd scurry like crazy to deliver that promise.

But this certificate business was meant to be a bit of frivolity, not a job. Clyde was spending too much time printing, framing and stuffing envelopes. *My talent*, he told himself, *is ideas, not licking envelopes.*

It was time for a coffee and another think.

When he began his PR career, believe it or not, he sent out press releases by telex. He would sit at the machine and punch a tape then feed it through the sprockets as it sent the news to the various newspapers. The newspaper had the same telex machine which received the message and printed it out. The cadet reporters would rip the paper off the machine and hand it to the news editor.

Then one day as Clyde sat at the telex machine punching in a news release, a consultant came to him with a direct-mail leaflet.

Look at this, she said. *It's a machine called a Fax. You put the typed news release into it, and at the same time it comes out at the newspaper."*

Bullshit, Clyde said, continuing to punch the telex tape. *How could that ever work?*

Six months later the telex was dead, and everyone used faxes. Now the fax is dead, and we use email.

But the lesson is important. You grasp technology and use it to your advantage. First, he had to avoid the framing costs and effort.

Clyde went online and changed the ISOCC offer to *'$180 for a signed, printed certificate, easily frameable.'* Then he thought about printing, mailing costs, and envelope stuffing and he changed it again to *'$180 delivered online ready for printing and framing to suit your décor.'* Then he went back and changed it to *'$185 for your color certificate, delivered online ready for printing and framing to suit your décor.'* The addition of color was, of course, free now that his days of paper printing, packing and posting were behind him.

Then Clyde noticed that he had mail. His rolling campaign sending out releases with certificates was working. Forty-five more orders! $6,480, at the old rate. $8,325 at the new.

He prepared 45 emails with color certificates as attachments. He added the draft media releases for nothing. And added that when they paid for their certificate, they would also get free membership of the ISOCC. Something for nothing. Added value. A bonus.

It took him four hours to change and insert names and addresses, a god-forsaken task if ever there was one. He'd have to think of a better way.

Social media had always been a mystery to him. He knew that most people, including him, had a Facebook account for looking at pictures of grandchildren, but while social media delivered quantity, there was seldom quality. It was, however, cheap to access, so Clyde went into Bigpond, Hotmail, Gmail, Live, TPG and Yahoo and opened free email accounts for Annie and himself and for their daughters. Then he went into on to Trip Advisor, Expedia, Yahoo! Travel, Booking, Priceline, Travelocity, Lonely Planet, Fodors and Wikitravel and opened membership for each new email address. And over the next few hours, he gave all his recipients a huge wrap for their coffee. Now his clients (none of whom knew of him) were getting some serious coverage, in both local media and online.

Finally, he wrote to each new member congratulating them on their coverage and sending them to the appropriate websites. Another rule, never let a client miss seeing a benefit. Take the credit, even if you weren't actually involved.

Then he went down to the beach and had another latte. All that had taken another three days. Too long.

CHAPTER SEVEN: The power of praise

But what a hoot! Everybody was a winner. There was something visceral about the human need for acknowledgment and Clyde was addressing it using something as old-hat as a certificate, delivered in a modern, cost-effective manner.

That intrinsic need for recognition went back to childhood. Everyone valued a certificate from school, whether for running or mathematics, art or reading. A certificate gave you a warm feeling. You felt good and so did your family. You were special. To whatever degree, you'd arrived and been recognised. The certificate was the authentic documentation of your success. It was tangible. It was proof. You held it in your hand or hung it on the wall, and it remained there unlike a fleeting mention online. Insurance salespersons hung them on the wall. Charities gave them out to donors. Travel agents got them for selling a distributor's product. Universities gave them for years of hard toil.

Framed and hung somewhere obvious, the certificate became an on-going, positive part of life, reinforcement of how well you'd done.

The International Society of Coffee Connoisseurs was now authentic. The coffee lounges had not only been awarded certificates and but they'd gained valuable help in promoting their businesses. Their recognition gave them a competitive edge in the market. Even their customers were proud that they'd chosen to drink their macchiato in an internationally-recognised establishment. *It is*, thought Clyde, *the world's cheapest PR.*

As far as he knew, he was breaking no laws. In fact, the way he figured it, anyone could give anyone else a certificate. Perhaps the Society had been a bit of a stretch, but now it was registered and therefore official. It had a website. The next step would be to grow it into something that nobody could doubt had the gravitas inherent in its name.

Small business starts off tiny, he thought, *with its self-promotion far exceeding its actual capability. Then as it grows, its abilities expand and suddenly it's no longer exaggerating. We need to accept this fact if small business is to become something bigger,* he mused. *We need to turn a blind eye, give a wry grin and move on. The world's best pies! A family company! Unmatched design! Nothing comes close! A tradition going back 2 years!*

Who cares if their claims are BIG. They're having a go. They're trying to grow. Let them be.

Clyde's situation was no different from that of any small business or any person pretending to be a bit bigger and more exciting than they actually were. Who hadn't exaggerated when selling their house? He remembered his father, who'd been a very successful real estate agent, telling him how he'd been invited to a house by the owner who claimed it was a bungalow with sea views. The only sight of the harbor was a glimpse gained by standing on the toilet seat and peering through the louvre windows. Were all real estate agents shonky? No way. Did car sellers make wild claims? Not always.

It almost made Clyde indignant to consider any negative side to what he was doing. He kept telling himself that he had every right to run an International Society of Coffee Connoisseurs because, well, he liked coffee. It was international, technically, because he'd issued certificates in two countries. It had a website! You didn't have to be a recognised coffee afficionado to run a Society of Coffee Connoisseurs. After all, people who managed rugby clubs didn't necessarily play rugby. People who administered hospitals were not all doctors.

And now he had members, some of whom actually made coffee for a living. The blogs on the website had a healthy ring to them as Clyde's family discussed what made a good cappuccino, latte, macchiato. Yes, most of the blogs were from Annie, their two daughters, and Clyde, but they were coffee lovers too, except for Annie.

Social media works because people want to be a part of something bigger than themselves. They want to feel they can contribute and be listened to. Blogs do that. They bond people together with a shared interest. Clyde could use that!

He improved the website by providing more background. *The ISOCC does not represent the interests of any commercial coffee brand. It is a not-for-profit organization whose members enjoy coffee. We are proud to be able to give recognition to those baristas and coffee bar/lounge-owners who have set out to make the best coffee for their customers.* He asked questions like: *How important is it to support green coffee bean growers?* He called for members. *Free to coffee lovers,* it said. *Just supply your name on the attached form, and if you know of a coffee lounge that you believe deserves recognition, please supply the name.*

You should always be selling. A missed opportunity is simply that. Missed forever.

The ISOCC had a website and it was now a legitimate Society. It didn't take a lot to add some real clout. Many years ago, just before Gerry had fired him from his boating magazine using someone else to do it, Clyde had written a front-page article in Cruising Helmsman on the dangers posed to yachtsmen by piracy. He'd walked into The Daily Herald library and spent an hour copying stories from old editions. Then he plagiarised those articles and wrote a powerful feature on the dangers international yachtsmen faced when sailing through Indonesia and Somalian waters, quoting from article after article, with great authority. The magazine sales went up by at least 15 copies that month and something even more astonishing happened. One copy must have been purchased by a journalist working on the Daily Herald. Two weeks after the magazine's publication Clyde was reading the Saturday edition of the Herald and found a half-page feature article on Piracy. And there in the third paragraph, it read: *Editor of Cruising Helmsman Magazine Clyde West says areas to be avoided include...* It went on to quote Clyde extensively. So the Herald was quoting Clyde quoting articles from The Herald. Another lesson. Once published, material is usually free to be used. Today you don't need to go to a newspaper library; you just go online. There is endless information on websites and it's usually free.

That gave Clyde another idea. He Googled 'Coffee Production'. And there they were, the world's top coffee producers: Brazil was the champion with 42,500,000 bags a year, then

Vietnam 15,000,000, Colombia 11,600,000, Indonesia 6,850,000, Ethiopia 6,500,000 … and so it went on.

He copied the list, changed a few words just in case there was copyright involved, and put it on the website. A nice bit of credibility.

Wikipedia told him: *Coffee is an important commodity and a popular beverage. Over 2.25 billion cups of coffee are consumed in the world every day.[1] Over 90 percent of coffee production takes place in developing countries, while consumption happens mainly in the industrialized economies.[1]*

Worldwide, 25 million small producers rely on coffee for a living. For instance, in Brazil alone, where almost a third of all the world's coffee is produced, over 5 million people are employed in the cultivation and harvesting of over 3 billion coffee plants; it is a much more labour-intensive culture than alternative cultures of the Colletone regions as sugar cane or cattle, as it is not subject to automation and requires constant attention.

Coffee is also bought and sold as a commodity on the New York Board of Trade. This is where coffee futures contracts are traded, which are a financial asset involving a standardized contract for the future sale or purchase of a unit of coffee at an agreed price. The world's largest transfer point for coffee is the port of Hamburg, Germany."

Clyde put it up on his site with a credit. He emailed the Corporate Affairs Department at one of the world's big Italian coffee brands and told them he wished to celebrate their brand on the International Society of Coffee Connoisseurs website. He sent them the section of their own website he wished to use and received a nice email from Francesca Bellesconi, assistant PR officer, giving him permission.

He wrote a new section for the ISOCC site: *The World's Great Coffee Brands. From time to time the ISOCC will be celebrating the achievements of great coffee brands from around the world. This month we look at one of the world's greatest.'*

Then he downloaded the material from their website.

There was a lot of information, and some of it was dull, so he left much out.

But now he had a site that added value, education, and interest as well as certificates. It hadn't had many hits yet, but it had at least a modicum of depth.

The lesson? Information today, about anything, is cheap or free, and plentiful. You don't have to create anymore, just copy from the web, where there is too much information anyway. Research is something that is done by others these days. Plagiarism is becoming initiative.

CHAPTER EIGHT: We Go National!

Meanwhile, was Clyde becoming a genuine coffee aficionado? He told himself yes, but probably not. Was he having fun? You bet!

He emailed every certificate holder and suggested they go to the upgraded ISOCC website. He recommended they also get their customers to give them a plug on Trip Advisor and all the other travel sites. He suggested they launch a promotion for customers, with every sixth coffee free, provided the customer went online and signed up for membership of the ISOCC.

A week later he wrote to the ISOCC's growing membership with what was to become the first of many small business improvement tips. He told them if they had not had an official opening for their coffee lounge, they should at least have a one year anniversary, or five years or ten, or the millionth customer or whatever they could arrange. *Invite the customers, invite the media and have a local dignitary make a speech. If you can't get the Premier, get a minister, if you can't get one of them get the local member or a sports star, or the mayor or a councilor, (they'll turn up to anything) or get anybody else worthy of a picture. And think like a photographer. Create a picture. Get a cute dog to lick a latte, or a cute kid to sip a baby chino. Think cute because cute sells.*

To hell with not wanting work or money. Clyde was hooked and he took the marketing up a notch. He reminded himself again that he was, after all, helping small businesses with tiny budgets who did not know how to promote themselves. A worthy cause! But just in case it went too well, he went back to the website and deleted the words *not-for-profit*.

The Yellow Pages Directory online led him to the names of 3,200 coffee lounges in each of Australia's capital cities. He spent two days when he was not filling certificate orders, collating their email addresses and preparing a covering letter:

Dear Owner,

Congratulations! The International Society of Coffee Connoisseurs has recognised your business as serving the Best Coffee in XXXXXX. The draft of an easily-frameable signed color certificate is attached, which recognises the quality of your coffee. Please check that your details are correct on the certificate. The cost of the color certificate for one year is $198. On receipt of your funds, you may print it out and *frame it in a manner that suits your décor. Also attached is a story for your local newspapers.*

Visit our website at www.ISOCC.com.au. Should you recommend us to others, you will receive your next annual certificate free, should you qualify for it. Don't forget to sign up as a Society member. It's free!

> *Signed*
>
> *(Totally illegible signature)*
>
> *CEO*
>
> *ISOCC*

In his days, a direct mailer was successful if it generated a response of more than 2 or 3 percent. He received nearly 7 percent return - a stunning two hundred and twenty-three certificates ($44,154). He presumed some would have just printed the certificate without paying, but that was to be expected.

The ISOCC was truly national as well as international. And he was growing a little rich.

Clyde put it down to the incredible power of coffee generally. Coffee lounges do not have customers; they have devotees. If you treat your customers as experts, they stay with you, and his were staying with him.

He rang Gerry in Barbados.

Gerry, do you remember when we gave Sam that certificate?

Yeah, it's still on the wall.

Remember I made you Chairman?

Of course, it's a title I shall cherish forever. What's the Society again?

It's the International Society of Coffee Connoisseurs. Do you still want to be Chairman?

Why?

Well, I think it could become a paid gig.

Clyde explained what he was doing.

Shit! That's crazy.

Yes, but fun, and legal and helpful and I'm going to keep going.

Do I have to do anything?

Not a lot, just go online and become a member www.ISOCC.com.au But you deserve a reward. As Chairman you should have a monthly stipend. Of course, nobody will know you are Chairman except you and me, but it's a paid position.

How much?

"Let's agree that in return for services delivered, namely inviting us to Barbados, you'll get a stipend of $300 per month, which you must spend only on food and wine.

Really? Can we afford that?

What do you mean WE? You haven't accepted yet."

Ok, I don't give a shit.Sign me up.

(Gerry cannot count being a motivational speaker among his many accomplishments)

Leave the money to me, said Clyde. *If it doesn't work out, you'll get nothing, and if it does, you get dinner!*

Done!

Time to market some more.

Clyde launched a national PR campaign by writing a total of 1670 letters on his new ISOCC letterhead (designed on PowerPoint, total time 13 minutes), one letter to each regional and suburban newspaper and community magazine covering the suburb of the coffee lounges to which he'd sent a certificate, advising them that ISOCC had issued a certificate to the local businesses and asking if a local story might be warranted. One hundred and twenty-seven newspapers ran stories. Clyde added local radio stations and they ran 62 items, according to

Media Monitors, which he now used to follow the ISOCC's media stardom. Every media exposure was recorded on the ISOCC website, by Annie, who whinged a lot.

Clyde was on a roll. He couldn't sleep. Adrenalin surged. He felt 30 again! When the local newspapers and radio stations went online, they found an ISOCC website that had significant credibility, more than enough to let them run the story.

He created an ISOCC Facebook page and every few days put up another winner's certificate. Again, the web made it simple. The coffee lounges' own websites invariably contained Facebook links. ISOCC quickly had 500 followers and growing. Clyde launched the *Name the best coffee in your suburb* campaign. ISOCC quickly grew to 3,800 followers and 600 more coffee lounge members.

Clyde created a site on LinkedIn. He'd previously thought LinkedIn was of value only to people looking for jobs, but it was easy enough to belong and that's the lesson of the web: It's easy, so do it.

And the orders kept coming, first 10 a day, then 25, then once the national campaign had hit, more than 35 orders a day. In one crazy month, he printed and emailed 1,050 certificates worth

$194,250. The bank account contained $640,000.

Young Ivan, the bank manager, was ecstatic. Every time Clyde visited Ivan told him that he spent a lot of time on the ISOCC website. He asked if Clyde needed to borrow money and looked very upset when he said no. Clyde explained that the only reason you need money is because you have overheads and Clyde had decided his business should not have those.

Overheads are the death of business, he decided. He'd run companies which spent 95 percent of their revenue servicing their own overheads. He'd tell people jokingly that he ran a not-for-profit enterprise and at times he did. How crazy is that! Other businesses strive to make a mere 12 percent profit and celebrate when they do.

Overheads had to be avoided and so did getting trapped by too much menial work. Due to his new role as fulfilment officer, Clyde was getting close to hitting the wall. His ears started to whistle endlessly. He was snowed under, getting up each day at 5 am, using his (admittedly brand new) deluxe coffee machine, then hitting the (admittedly brand new) computer. By 10 pm he was exhausted. Not to mention his better half was proving better at complaining than just being better.

Time for some more thinking.

Clyde was determined not to take on overheads. *As simple as can be but no simpler,* was Einstein's catch-cry, passed on to him by an old buddy David (who unashamedly claimed it as his own). If it was good enough for Albert, it would be good enough for the ISOCC.

But he couldn't both service this business and grow it. He needed people with time on their hands. Cost-effective people. And he had to find a means of not having them as employees.

Clyde ran an advertisement in the local newspaper and interviewed until he'd short-listed five housewives with computers. He hired four to send emails from their homes, with releases, letters, and certificates attached.

Their briefing took three hours. They received $2.50 for each certificate sent. It was a huge 'overhead' but not really. He only had to pay them after they'd generated the income. He'd avoided the pitfall of having to pay staff even when they did not generate revenue. If they goofed off, then Clyde did not have to pay them. He felt a little like a piece-meal sweat-shop owner, but there was a huge difference: His women could earn $60 an hour, at home, working the hours that suited them. The four emailers seemed thrilled and why not? That's $480 a day or $2,400 a week; $100,000-plus for a year, even with a week or so for holidays.

"I'm helping struggling mums pay their way," he told himself. He felt even more altruistic - a good Samaritan! He put up the cost of the certificates to $200.

"But," he thought, *"I need to be very clear in my goal setting. I don't want to run a business or pay superannuation, insurances, holiday pay, sick pay and such, because I know that will distract me from any strengths I might have."*

He had his accountant, at Clyde's cost, help the email mums form a company between them. Their company would send the accountant one invoice each month. He would pay the bill due to their company. Then they'd pay their personal taxes from the combined proceeds before distributing the rest. In time, for their own tax purposes they would need other clients, but for now, that would work.

Still no direct overheads as such. Still, everyone actually delivered results. No secretaries, receptionists, office leases.

All Clyde's overheads were linked to the level of revenue. If there was no work, the overheads stopped. He wished he'd thought of it years ago.

The fifth housewife was Michelle and she already worked from home helping people with their websites. She had her own company and took over the ISOCC website enhancement for

$700 a week. Another invoice, but still no employees. As long as he added new members and issued certificates, he could keep paying the bills, and if the income dried up, the bills stopped too. Michelle's brief was to surf the web for information about coffee, then load the best of it on to the ISOCC site, either quoting a source or changing it enough to avoid copyright issues. Unethical? It used to be. Now it's called research.

There was a bonus, too. Each time Michelle did her work she enhanced the site, meaning search engines found it easier and quicker. The busier the site became, the more the search engines would find it.

Clyde went back to Nigel and had him make a specific change to the website. He created some areas of white space in the site and then using white type, so the text would be invisible, he filled each area with hidden words, like Lavazza, coffee, cappuccino, latte, Starbucks, Baristas, The Coffee Club, Gloria Jeans and 150 other names of coffee chains and coffee brands. Why? Because when people searched the web for one of those names, using Google or Yahoo or any engine, the ISOCC site might be found, because it contained the keyword they'd used in their search. Illegal? Not from Clyde's experience. Unethical? Usually but not in this case, because it didn't harm anyone. Was the trick used elsewhere? Yes, it'd been done to Clyde when he ran a previous business.

A former employee had created her own site and buried Clyde's name and his company's name in a blank space on her site, white on white, invisible on her website unless you knew how to find it. On the same pages, she also hid text with the name of every program owned by her competitors. Clyde had discovered it when he Googled 'Clyde West' and her company name came up, with his name mentioned in the introduction. What made it even more curious was that when he went to her site, there was no mention of him or his company in the readable text. But Nigel found it hidden white-on-white in blank spaces throughout her site. He complained to Google that she was trading off someone else's name, and they wrote to her. Did she stop? Eventually, but only after Clyde shamed her by contacting all clients and former employees.

Still, this time Clyde was not trading off anyone - a big difference. Unlike his 'not-to-be-named-but-you-know-who-you-are employee' none of the names he used were actual competitors because he didn't have any, so ironically he was helping others promote their businesses, too. He could live with that.

After a month, when anyone typed the word 'coffee' into the search engines, the ISOCC came up on page 2, then on page 1. ISOCC was a force to be reckoned with, web-wise anyway. Clyde had maximised the effectiveness of his website.

CHAPTER NINE: People Problems

Don't you hate dealing with people? Within six short months, Clyde's four email housewives claimed they were working too many hours in their little company. One resigned to spend more time with the baby, and the others asked for more money. More money!

People problems. Not again! Clyde had had his share of dealing with people and refused to start doing that again. As Gerry had done with him, he asked someone else (Peter his accountant) to fire them. He understood they didn't take it well, but they'd started it by being pushy. He was too old to be shoved around by anyone.

There had to be a better way.

Only Michelle had stayed on doing her web enhancement with endless reliability and talent. Clyde gave her a raise as much to spite the other four as to reward her diligence.

But he decided that too much website information could be too much of a good thing, so he made a note to cut back the website upgrades to once every three months. Michelle would still be happy, and he would lower his overheads.

Once more he rang Nigel, his former IT guru from another life. Nigel now lived on the Coromandel Peninsula in New Zealand and ran IT for Clyde's old company two days a week.

The international tones sounded and after half a dozen rings Clyde heard fumbling, clicking and the roar of an engine in the background.

"Hullo," said a flustered voice.

"Nigel! It's Clyde. West."

"Hi mate, how are you?"

"Bloody hell, what's that noise in the background?"

"It's my outboard. I'm fishing. Let me turn it off.

"That's better. What's up?"

"Do you need a bit of work?"

"Sure, what is it?"

With seagulls squawking in the background, he listened as Clyde asked him to create a software program that could automatically generate a tailored certificate, a media release, and an invoice.

"What's the budget?"

"I trust you, Nigel. It will be what it costs."

"I'll need some mates. Give me a couple of weeks," he said.

He did it in three. Plus he added an automatic receipt to go out once the money had been banked. As in the past, Clyde had trusted him and he'd delivered. He sent him $25,000. He was worth it. Nigel bought a new outboard.

Now ISOCC could service the inflow of requests by having Annie type in a name and region and pressing a button. The computer would then generate the tailored certificate, in color, the media release mentioning the suburb and an invoice. When the cash arrived, it would send a receipt. There were teething problems, but Nigel sorted them.

Ready, Fire, Aim is the best way to move quickly, said Clyde. Not ready, aim, adjust, adjust, adjust... (now where did that target go?)

But even changing the names was an onerous task and one that would only get worse as the business kept growing. It was a waste of time to do the boring work. And Annie was getting more and more vocal.

I'm not doing it, Clyde told himself. I'm an ideas man – ever humble but an ideas man.

An old friend and business partner had once taught him that there are three types of people in the world: Initiators, Administrators, and

Stoppers. He said some people were initiators; they created, came up with brilliant ideas – and were usually hopeless at running businesses or stopping bad business practices. The Administrators were those who ran businesses superbly but seldom had brilliant ideas, nor were they great at stopping things. Stoppers were the people you brought in to fix things, to fire people, to cut businesses to the bone – but everyone ended up hating them and would refuse to work with them into the future.

Yes, Clyde was an initiator! *"An ideas man,"* he thought. That was his great strength and he'd get others to do the running and stopping.

He didn't want to run staff because he'd have to talk to them, and Annie had responded in two brisk words when he suggested she might like to continue handling the fulfilment side of things. But the day-to-day servicing of the certificate/PR business was stultifying. *"I'm going to have to find a better way,"* he said.

Even the website was threatening to run the business rather than helping communication. Michelle was doing a brilliant job under trying circumstances, as Clyde demanded more and more depth to the ISOCC site, more blogs, more comment, more interactivity, more posting of certificate winners and media clippings. She was soldiering on but crying for help. Even the fact that she was now earning $3,000 a week (she hadn't asked for more) didn't help the fact that she physically could not meet the needs of bloggers and the insatiable craving for new information on the website. Like so many websites, the site was taking over their lives.

"The trouble with websites," Clyde told Michelle, *"is that I have yet to meet someone who is happy with their own one. Websites are an endless journey, not a finite tool. Their avarice for words and cash is beyond belief, thus trillions are spent online. I wonder how many of those trillions are actually contributing value to society."*

The ISOCC site was becoming a burden with which Clyde would have to deal, he thought (noting that he'd cleverly avoided the use of a dangling participle). He sat down with Michelle and cut back the workload. The site was now, by any standards, a substantial venue for anything to do with coffee. The occasional new material would be enough for a while.

Bookkeeping was also getting scary, so he rang accountant Peter and did a deal. Peter hired a full-time bookkeeper and took over the money side of things entirely. Clyde knew how much was coming in, but Peter's firm collected and banked it. He sent Clyde a bigger invoice and a monthly report. Clyde saved time doing books, which he told himself no entrepreneur should ever do.

But he was not a happy camper. On the positive side, Annie and he were the entire company, with minimal invoices to pay and no annoying partners or employees. But against that, there was too much work and he was not sure he was delivering real value to each client. He knew that to service his clients superbly he should have been placing recommendations for every single recipient on Trip Advisor, Facebook, LinkedIn and a host of other food and travel sites. Of course, the members still only paid $200, so anything extra was costing him money.

But over-servicing was second nature to him and it had never let him down in the past, but this extra work alone took hours. He had a significant workload building up and nobody, except a very reluctant wife, to do the work.

Then over the top of her Peroni glass, Annie announced her early retirement due to '*personal issues*'.

"*Personally, I'm not bloody well doing it,*" she said.

God, it's hard to get good help!

Perhaps it was time to pull the plug. "*I never signed up for this,*" he cursed. "*I'm meant to be retired and relaxed.*"

And then the telephone rang.

Someone forgettable once said: *"There's no such thing as luck... only being in the right position."* The right position for Clyde was three rings from the phone, in his recliner, Gewurztraminer in one hand and remote in the other.

CHAPTER TEN: We Get Some Help

Clyde prized himself out of the recliner and rolled to the left to grab the handset:

"Good evening Mr. Best," said an Indian voice. *"My name is Rajik. I wonder if I may call you Clive?"*

Here we go. Another pestering Indian call-centre person ringing at dinner time and getting all his details wrong. Clyde didn't have a whistle to blow down the line, so he resorted to sarcasm, fuelled by wine:

"Call me Clive? Of course, you can Ramjet," he said, resorting to smart arse. Just as he'd done so many times in the past, he'd live to regret the flippant comment, but it didn't stop him. *"You can call me anything you like, Rachet."*

"I am wondering if you are happy with your current life insurance coverage?"

"I am actually," Clyde replied. Then whether it was the wine or the stress, he paused for a second.

"Listen Rammie, can I talk to your boss, about a business opportunity?"

There was a slight delay and a new voice came on.

"Good evening Mr. Best. My name is Ramesh. Do you have a problem with which I may assist?"

"I do, actually. Are you the boss?"

"I am very proudly the owner, and I promise you that I am here to serve. How can I help you?

"Well, Ramesh, first up, my name is Clyde, not Clive, and my surname is West. As in direction."

"Oh my goodness. I am so sorry. I will have my team make the correction immediately."

"No worries, Ramesh," Clyde said. *"That's not why I wanted to talk to you. I think we may be able to do business together. Do you have a few minutes?"*

And over the next hour, he explained what the ISOCC needed.

"I can assure you that will not be a problem," Ramesh said. *"Can I come back to you by email with a proposition?"*

Twenty-seven days later Clyde had a team of diligent Mumbai Indian folk filling out the names on the computer-generated certificates and media releases at the cost of $1.80 each certificate and posting all Facebook, LinkedIn and Trip Advisor comments for the same rate.

"I love it!" he thought. *"I've a world without boundaries. I've got a virtual business!"*

So much for his Newport housewives.

This could work out nicely. Ramesh and his Mumbai Army would handle fulfilment and Peter's bookkeeper would count the dosh, while Clyde would drink coffee and fine wine and create exciting new plans.

Clyde rang Gerry, who'd returned to Budapest.

"I think you could be eating free dinners for a while," he told him.

"Be careful. It sounds too good to be true. And you know what that means."

"It is too good to be true. But it's fun. I think I've found the one thing in the world that needs the particular experience I have. There are a lot of people out there who need access to local newspapers and radio. I've done that. They need someone to write about them. I've done that for a living. They need marketing. I've built companies and run PR companies. They need creativity, and I have it. They need communication. I've taught it."

"Just be careful. You may think you're having fun, but you're meant to be retired."

"Oh listen to you, the man who went from publisher to sand miner!"

But Gerry was right, of course, Clyde knew he could have relaxed and just let the business generate a nice little income, but he was on a roll. And he liked a challenge. Experience had also taught him that if you're not growing, you're shrinking; standing still was not an option. *"If you ever find yourself managing a business day after day, it's time to get someone else to do it,"* he said to himself out loud. *"Your job should be pioneering, not farming."*

There were two logical means to grow this particular business exponentially. The first was to go international. Clyde would save the second, the scariest, for later.

He explained to Annie, what was involved. She sipped her second Peroni and poured him another Gewurz.

"Do you really want to do this?"

"I think I do. Funnily enough, I'm helping people. They can't afford to publicize themselves and I know how. $200 isn't much for the PR I give each of them."

"It is when you multiply it by 100,000," she said, wisely. *"That would be $20 million."*

Boy, did they laugh over that one!

And the ISOCC went international.

CHAPTER ELEVEN: The Power of the Web

Clyde couldn't believe how easy it was. He'd grown up in the days of typewriters, telephone books, and international directory assistance. The ability to look up anything in another country simply did not exist. But now he brewed himself a coffee and Googled 'coffee lounges' and the name of English-speaking world cities. Up came the lounges and he chose at random, one from each suburb. He found lounges in Los Angeles, San Francisco, Chicago and New York. He threw in Auckland and Wellington, and Christchurch. Then London and the rest of the British cities then crossed the Atlantic and hit Toronto and every other Canadian city. And then he threw in Singapore, (because he wouldn't mind getting into Asia.)

Now he'd proven it could be done it was time to pass the task on to the experts.

He rang Ramesh, then wrote him a simple marketing plan. Ramesh's team would do the research, pick the prospects, contact them, fill out the certificates, find the local papers and send the media releases. Clyde would be available, but seldom.

They agreed that to avoid any mistakes down the line Clyde would also create for Ramesh's people a train-the-trainer manual, another talent he'd gained in the consulting business. In his 26 years as a trainer, he'd written or had written probably fifty TTT manuals, covering such disciplines as Presentation Skills, Sales, Negotiation, Media Skill, Crisis Management, Leadership. Each had been used by his senior trainers to teach groups of consultants how to run workshops on the different subjects.

Ramesh had too many people who needed training so he'd developed a coterie of trusted coaches who taught smaller groups. And they needed the TTT manual. It took Clyde six days to write but it would turn out to be worth every second.

'*SELLING THE ISOCC*' was a very basic How to Do It manual, with the ISOCC copyright on the bottom of every page.

It opened with an explanatory page, which set the objectives and went on to teach people how to train others to sell the ISOCC Certificate to businesses in other countries, both online and, for the future, on the telephone.

Overkill it was not because he'd learned the hard way that unless people stick exactly to the best methodology, the impact is lost, problems occur, and objectives are not met. The civilisations that survive write things down. It's the same with companies, even small businesses. If it's only in your head and you fall sick, then things stop happening. If it's written down, you can leverage your IP by having others earn money for you.

And just as essential, was Clyde's realization that lawyers are rich for a very good reason. On the base of every page of every document Clyde produced, was the copyright symbol, the ISOCC and the year. On its own, it didn't do much but combined with licenses and contracts and letters from lawyers with expensive-sounding names – combined with all of those, sometimes just sometimes it was possible to defend your IP.

Lawyers are costly, but spending a few thousand at the start of any commercial relationship could save legal battles costing millions later. Just like a marriage, Clyde knew, there was endless trust at the beginning but if it went bad, good intentions and good nature went out the window.

Clyde had made sure that his friendships with Peter, Michelle, Ramesh, and Nigel, were underpinned with formal agreements that would last beyond comradeship.

With that manual and a few hours answering questions by phone, followed by Ramesh's in-house training sessions in Mumbai, the ISOCC took off in a most unexpected manner. Clyde had planned on a slowish start, but Ramesh had people, talented people with a work ethic. Not only did they find the clients, but they filled out the certificates and checked detail. Clyde suddenly realised why the world's multi-nationals used Indian call centres.

The Mumbai team took total charge of outbound marketing, with the single objective of contacting coffee lounges in every country, city, suburb, and town, everywhere in the English-speaking world.

That, of course, meant one lounge per suburb because Clyde wanted his members to gain an edge over their competitors. Exclusivity is a powerful sales tool. And exclusivity in a single suburb is enough because the competitors that harm your business are often only in the same suburb.

Each recipient was given free membership to the society, as well. It cost nothing and was added value.

Recipients received an email with their draft certificate with a generic story for the local newspaper and news tips to the local radio stations.

When Nigel complained that the extra work and fine-tuning was interfering with his fishing time, Clyde sent him another $20,000, a box of 2010 Hunter Vineyard Cabernet Sauvignon and told him to resign from all his other work.

Over the next four months, the international business snowballed.

We tend to think that opportunity lies in our suburb, our city, our State, our country, but if we really want to grow, we should only consider operating in the whole world. It's a big place, and in this case, filled with lots of cafes and coffee lounges. What worked in one country seemed to work in every English-speaking country. Coffee's appeal was ubiquitous.

Clyde had plenty to keep him busy when the outbound marketing campaign went berserk. Lounge after lounge, in country after country, signed up and paid their money. Insane? Yes, but Clyde had lucked out with a simple idea and a powerful marketing tool. Every element of the business plan worked together; the desperate need for small business to market itself; the emotional power of a certificate; the backing of an apparently massive global coffee society (just check the website); and the old-fashioned strength of local publicity. And behind it all the astounding power of recognition.

Clyde sat back stunned as the cogs meshed and the money flowed in, with minimal personal involvement. Each new lounge was found by the Mumbai team, approached automatically online and sold with the heartfelt excitement of a chance to have a real (color) certificate. Each request received was fulfilled with a mainly IT solution and the funds were recorded and banked.

Better still, the web was proving to be discreet, in that no certificate holder knew how many other certificates had been issued. Michelle published the ISOCC membership figures, but not the certificate numbers so nobody could easily find out what a money-spinner the ISOCC had become.

But raging success often leads to a fraying of the edges. Clyde's over-riding philosophy was that he was not going to have overheads, nor run anything himself. But Nigel and Peter started to phone when they had a question.

This has to be stopped, Clyde told Annie. I'm not here to answer other people's questions. He had Annie ring them both and explain that Clyde was no longer available for answers. He wanted them to find their own answers. He was far too busy doing other things – like finding ways to make them richer.

Small businesses that find themselves doing well often make the mistake of boasting about their success. It can be a terrible error. By all means, boast about what you do, but not your success at doing it. Best that every award winner knew of only a few others, not the reality that the certificates were floating down like confetti on thousands of delighted small business owners. If everyone knew that everyone had one, what would be the attraction?

One warm November evening Annie looked over Clyde's shoulder as he checked the ISOCC account. It was one of those mind-blowing moments. The debit column was virtually empty but there in the credit column, right at the bottom of page 7 was the revenue line: $4.7million! Twenty-six thousand five hundred certificates issued, and not one bit of framing, wrapping, posting involved. And only relatively minor costs of delivery.

Good God! This was extraordinary. He now had an expanding global business based on $200 units of sale, with no direct employees, paying three invoices a month. As his granddaughter, Tayla, would say: *"GET-OUT-OF-TOWN!!!!"*

The International Society of Coffee Connoisseurs had 27,800 registered members, with certificates issued to 26,700 coffee lounges. It also held a significant database for anyone who wanted to reach coffee lovers, something that had not escaped Clyde.

International was booming as our outbound marketing team in Mumbai targeted coffee lounges in each suburb in each major city, then mid-range cities and finally country towns. Of no surprise at all, the coffee lounges got more publicity in the country towns, because the local editors were prouder of their residents. Some things never change.

It had been fifteen months and Clyde was riding a bucking monster. Each day brought new orders, hundreds of them.

Annie and he sat down to a crayfish and champagne dinner on the terrace and mulled over what was happening.

She was the one person he could trust to still bring him down to earth.

He recalled 1993 when he had been a small part of the team that won the Olympic Games for Sydney. He'd flown back from Monte Carlo where he'd coached Sydney's winning presentation team. He was elated. Sydney had won the Olympic Games for the year 2000! He arrived home to hugs and kisses and Annie sat him down with a glass of champagne. He started to regale her the war stories of Monte Carlo: the famous people he'd mixed with, the kiss from Joan Sutherland, the hug from Anita Keating, handshake from the Prime Minister, the endless praise… He was, at least in his own mind, a hero!

And then Annie leaned in and whispered in his ear:

"It's rubbish bin night, dear."

And she was about to strike again.

"We can go on like this for ages!" Clyde said to Annie. *"It's a money-making machine. One certificate for one lounge in every suburb of the English-speaking world!"*

And she struck.

"You've forgotten something," she said.

"It's not rubbish bin night is it?"

"No, but it's been over a year and you can now sell another certificate to every member."

While Clyde had been roaring ahead at light speed, he'd been going too quickly. Everybody needs someone to sweep up after them. He'd been expanding so quickly he'd forgotten that each certificate only lasted one year. Now it was next year. It was over 12 months since the first certificate was issued in Barbados and it was time to test the resilience of what he'd built. It's easy for someone to buy something once, but the true test of a good product is if someone will continue to buy it. He'd made the mistake that many make in business, he'd been picking the low-hanging fruit by adding new customers and not mining the existing customer base.

He kicked himself. Existing customers have already been sold. They weren't cold calls. They were hot, so why had he not kept his eye on them!

He drafted an email to the mainly-Australian certificate holders who had been members for a year or more and wrote:

'*Congratulations, the International Society of Coffee Connoisseurs has once again chosen your café for a certificate of excellence ... two years in a row! Your consistent success is something to be shared with all your customers. In recognition of your continued contribution to great coffee, the certificate cost for year two has been held to $200. Add the latest award to your existing certificate to demonstrate the on-going quality of your excellent coffee. Enclosed is an invoice for your next annual certificate. Please check it. As part of our service, we have prepared for you a media release which we suggest you forward to your local newspapers and magazines. Once again congratulations!*'
He signed it with the illegible flourish.

But sending reminders like this was a manual task, a boring manual task. In between landing schnapper, Nigel had his team build software, to automatically flag the anniversary of certificates 12 months to the day after they received their first award. With no human input at all the

ISOCC could now send out automatic renewal emails when due.

From Clyde's experience, the normal drop-off rate for renewals could be very high, so he needed Ramesh and his team to follow up. They flew to Mumbai, after a week in Koh Samui, Thailand. They landed and booked into a penthouse suite at the Hyatt Regency, Mumbai.

The next morning they met Ramesh in one of the hotel's many gilt-lined conference rooms.

They thrashed out a deal for the cost of telephone calls and his team agreed to ring every recipient after they had received their reminder. A huge job, but cost-effective nevertheless.

Ramesh was a good negotiator and he did an excellent deal for his company. But Clyde was an optimist and was more interested in growth than margins, so they were both happy. He was paying a little more, but it frankly did not matter. This new income was, incredibly, just play money. Clyde chose to pay more and have less stress.

It did not take long to see if the renewal campaign paid off.

CHAPTER TWELVE: People are your business

During the Mumbai meeting, Annie noticed Ramesh was fidgeting a bit and asked him what was wrong.

"Aaah, Mrs. Annie, I would be honoured if you and Mr. West would do me the honour and visit my premises to meet my humble team," he said.

And they did, that afternoon.

Ramesh picked them up by limo and they drove for twenty minutes, deep into the smelly chaos that is Mumbai, double-parking in a crowded, noisy street beside a grubby glass door. The outside of the building seemed to have been coated with telephone and power cables, haphazardly hooked together like spaghetti until the façade looked like it had been consumed by wild vines. Power lines were everywhere in the street, as were mopeds, bicycles, young people on phones and street vendors.

"Come, come," Ramesh said, ushering the pair two floors up a narrow flight of stairs as his chauffeur sat happily blocking the entire road.

Ramesh paused in the small foyer atop the second flight and opened another door with a flourish.

"Welcome to my company," he said, grinning.

They walked through to be met with deafening applause, from more than 200 people, none of whom seemed to be older than twenty-five.

Imagine a huge room filled with cubicles and PC's, cables everywhere. The hum of a generator somewhere close, motivational signs above every desk:

'Carpe Diem! Believe! Persistence! Achievement! Winners are Grinners! Life begins at the end of your comfort zone!'

They threaded their way through desks, shaking hands as the clapping continued and employees high-fived each other. Clyde made an impromptu speech thanking them for their exceptional work. *"You are helping thousands of small business owners around the world, to become successful,"* he said. And he suddenly realised that he meant it. These guys were doing as much or more than he had done to help small business. They took 150 selfies on iPhones and left humbled, flying home the next day confident that Ramesh and his team were gold.

By now, by just about any standards, the ISOCC had an impressive annual income stream. *"But we're one mile wide and one inch deep,"* he thought. *"It's a balloon and if someone pricks it, bang!"*

Clyde was determined to rise above any practices that might cast doubt on his authenticity. He wanted to be legitimate, not just legally, but ethically. So he added another layer of quality control by having his sister Lesley proofread everything published and/or sent to clients. She had retired and worked from her home, online, as you can do these days. Clyde paid for the fastest link available. It was a fulltime job for which her little company was very well paid.

Again, he avoided the need for offices.

And Clyde couldn't help casting his mind back to all the premises he'd opened at huge expense and then closed over the years in the course of building a global business. Auckland, Wellington, Brisbane, Perth, Adelaide, Bangkok, Singapore, Melbourne, Hong Kong, London, Toronto, Paris, San Francisco, Boston, New York, Dublin, Kuala Lumpur, Madrid, Athens, Lisbon, New Jersey, Chicago, all opened and many closed. Over twenty-five years he'd spent millions of dollars on real estate rented to hold employees. Now he had none. Having offices with all their overheads and people, in hindsight, had been totally stupid.

Clyde was also smashing some old business truisms. Advertising guru David Ogilvy had taught him an important lesson once (well, to be honest, it wasn't David, but a book he wrote). His advertising account directors used to carry around three cards, each with one word printed on them. One said 'QUALITY'. The second 'PRICE'. And the third 'TIME'. They would tell a client: "You can have any two, but not three."

In other words, if you wanted a quality job and you wanted it quickly, it would not be cheap. If you wanted a low price and quality, it would take longer and if you wanted a low price and quickly, quality would suffer.

With Lesley's help and that of Michelle and his Indian researchers, the quality was now there. Price had been kept really low, so if you were to believe Mr. Ogilvy, you would think time would be affected, but it wasn't. It wasn't because there were very few meetings. Clyde made decisions fast, and critically, he had the web. Ready, Fire, Aim! He'd have an idea, launch it and then adjust it if necessary. Even though he'd started issuing certificates before technically forming the Society, he now offered a quality service backed by a substantial website – and had done it without any financial investment.

So, he thought, we've proved Mr. Ogilvy wrong. We're delivering quality, low price, and speed. If Ogilvy had not been dead, I think I would have phoned him and explained that, given the power of the web and cheaper labour, he might have to re-think his famous quote.

Enormous sums of money were flowing in and the business was expanding exponentially with no staff coming to Clyde wanting more money, days off, a better place to sit, an iPad or a new title.

Of course, sometimes he found that he could have thought things through a little better. He'd grown supersonically and had chosen to reach one coffee lounge in each suburb, which left a lot without certificates. Greed led him to think of a way around that obstacle and he decided that the only thing stopping ISOCC from giving other cafés a certificate was the need for each recipient to have a competitive advantage. But what if the other lounges had a certificate from a **different** Society? Then they could win as well.

But avarice is a terrible thing. When he thought it through, there was a major flaw that could bring down everything he'd achieved. Journalists may be a bit lazy at times (he certainly had been), but they're not stupid. It wouldn't work because the local media would find it a bit tricky having every lounge receive a certificate from multiple societies. While Clyde didn't totally dismiss the option of creating other coffee societies, he parked it for later. It would, he decided, have been a major mistake. He'd dodged a bullet, and he just moved on.

Due to the successful renewal program, it seemed the ISOCC was more than a flash-in-the-pan. It was self-generating repeat business. No less than seventy-eight percent of its coffee lounges renewed their certificates for the following 12 months. ($4million plus)

Some did not renew and a few called the Society names, but Clyde ignored them. It was like drowning in money. He thought of the New Zealand drug king who had made love to his lawyer on a bed covered in bank notes. He even suggested the concept to Annie over drinks. Her snort and "Dream on" gave him little encouragement.

Did he have issues? Yes, but not many considering the income.

Most were just whiners and people with nothing better to do. One indignant lounge owner wrote a scathing email, which Clyde framed ($16, black). *"If you think for one second I'm going to send off $200 to some rat-bag outfit who will rip me off and give me nothing in return, you are very much mistaken,"* the prospect ranted. *"The certificate is badly designed and I recognise it as being straight from Microsoft art. Are you so damn cheap that you won't even have a decent certificate designed?"*

Clyde responded in two ways. First, he had his daughter Melinda, the graphic designer, create a much better-looking, color certificate. He kicked himself for not having done so earlier. Then he calmly wrote back to the complainant:

"Dear Sir, Thank you for your email, offering suggestions about the ISOCC Certificate program. We thank you for them. We regret to inform you that we have found on checking our records, your lounge did not meet the standards required for our certificate. Therefore the email you received was sent in error. We apologise for this error. We have now given the certificate to a business in your suburb which meets the standards required by our many thousands of members. If you would like to submit your name again for next year's award, we suggest you might look for improvement in the following areas: friendliness, customer service, overall decor, food quality and lack of top-rate barista skills. If these areas are addressed to our satisfaction, we will again consider your business."

I know, he told Annie, it was childish, but it felt good too.

The ISOCC Indian team forwarded all other complaints from paid-up members to Peter who refunded their money instantly with a generic note telling them the ISOCC was sorry they had decided not to continue and *'would they like to recommend another café in their area?'* That, and the fact that they hadn't paid much anyway, either shut them up or encouraged them to pay once more. But overall, the ISOCC didn't get many complaints, because it charged little and gave much. Some complained that they sent off the press release to their local papers and did not get a story, not understanding that PR is cheaper than advertising for a reason: There is a guarantee that your advertisement will run, but no guarantee that a story will.

There was the claim made in some blogs that the ISOCC chose lounges at random without any checking for quality. It hurt a little, mainly because it was true. Clyde countered it by having Michelle publish 685 real recommendations that members had sent in. You can say what you like, but 685 recommendations posted as examples are as good as a billion to anyone reading. They painted a very convincing picture of an organisation that did not just choose lounges. Nevertheless, Clyde changed the website to include a new section titled *"How We Choose Award Winners."*

"Certificate winners are chosen by a combination of members' recommendations and from research conducted by our own global team. If you wish to nominate a lounge owner, simply send their details including email address to: Mylounge@ISOCC.com."

If having the Mumbai army go through directories to find names and emails was not research, then what was?

CHAPTER THIRTEEN: As Simple As Can Be...

Now, a mate once told Clyde that building a business to $15m or $16m was not hard.

"The real challenge is building it from 15 to 30," Jim said, *"because you need to add people and systems and HR and accountants."*

Well, he was right about that particular business, but not about Clyde's new one. He was determined to have no employees, a goal made easier by Annie having resigned anyway. He would instead pay others and let them build their overheads and their companies. When Peter the accountant mentioned he was having issues with growth, Clyde told him to suck it up. As all accountants feel they must, Peter also said Clyde should hire people, take offices, expand. He told him he didn't want to.

'As simple as can be, but no simpler.' That was the motto.

Clyde would pay generous fees for services, but he refused to support dozens of employees who could goof off and surf the web. No room for oxygen thieves in this business. No room for whiners. Every dollar he spent had to produce direct results, or as near to direct as he could have. And that went for his suppliers, Peter, Nigel, Lesley, Ramesh, and Michelle.

He told them at every opportunity: *"Be wary of overheads. Only expand when you have too much work. Never hire in the hope the work will keep coming. Keep them focused only on delivering results. Don't hire that layer of middle management that costs and does not pay for itself. You do not need managers for HR, PR, company secretaries, in-house lawyers, supervisors. If you need advice, just buy it in. It's cheaper in the long run."*

Every word he passed on was based on a guiding value, a lesson from his past in PR when he'd literally turned grey in three years by hiring cheap people because he was cheap, then not trusting them to do their jobs because he couldn't trust them because they were cheap. Then doing their work himself, until he went grey. He must have sounded passionate because it didn't take a lot to encourage them to minimise the people.

But he did have a looming tax problem. He decided to pay $800 and have a coffee with the leading international tax adviser at KPMG.

"Yes," the senior partner said, *"We can set you up in a tax haven like the Cayman Islands, where there is no tax. It will cost less than $20,000 to do that."*

"Great!" said Clyde with a huge grin, *"Let's do it!"*

"Well first let me explain what will happen... The day we set you up in the Caymans, the tax department will go through everything you have ever done looking for unpaid tax. We'll fight that and probably win, but it will probably cost you $200,000. Then every six months from then on they will go through you again, and each time we will fight them and charge you $200,000."

"Let's not do it!" said Clyde, ordering another coffee.

Instead, he began to pay tax, lots of it. After all, on a turnover heading towards $10m and costs of $1m, there is a tax liability. But there is also a lot left over. He was definitely not a not-for-profit business.

It was time for another coffee and a think.

Incredibly, the beginning of the ISOCC venture had been issuing one certificate in one café in one town on one island in the Eastern Caribbean, a concept which started as a joke between mates. Something incredible had evolved, and along the way, the ISOCC had become legitimate and significant. Nobody could doubt its authenticity, given the number of members and the work it did to promote coffee and cafes. It was not huge but it was biggish. It represented coffee lovers around the world.

It started as a prank and had turned into a tank.

Now the ISOCC had expanded into most English-speaking countries including the USA, Canada, England, Ireland, Scotland, South Africa, and New Zealand and it had a toehold in the Caribbean. The USA alone was a gigantic money-spinner.

All those countries spoke English, so it had been relatively easy. Ahead lay all those which had their own languages: Europe, India, South America, Africa, Eastern Europe, the Middle East and Asia. Maybe a hundred countries if Clyde got it right. But it would not be as easy.

It was time for Stage Two of the international expansion phase of the ISOCC. And it would need a different business model.

CHAPTER FOURTEEN: Learn From Your Past Mistakes

Clyde poured another glass of his superb Gewurz (now winner of best in class in The Royal Easter Show Wine Competition) and the inevitable Peroni for Annie, and they watched the sun drop down behind the swimming pool as the boats swung slowly on their moorings in the Bay. Their home was no longer modest. They may have been discouraging overheads in business, but the same could not be said of their private life.

They'd purchased a small bungalow in one of the city's prettiest waterfront suburbs and started renovating the day they moved in. They lived in the third bedroom while the rest was upgraded.

With success come trappings, he told Annie, but only once you have the success.

When they'd started their management training business in the late '80s, it had been a franchise and they'd been a franchisee. They later became so successful they did a reverse takeover of the franchisor and became a franchisor with their own franchisees. Then Clyde took over or shut down the franchisees and created a partnership.

They'd been in the franchise business and knew its pitfalls and benefits.

"God help us if we have to run a bloody franchise system again," said Annie. *"We'll be back in the people business. Franchisees rip you off. They think copyright infringement is initiative!"*

"Yes, but what do we have to lose? We're looking for the icing, not the cake. If it fails, it fails. Who gives a poop? The secret is that we do not run it ourselves."

She was right as usual, but Clyde was right, too. Yes, he had been stung by franchisees in the past, but without massive investment, there was no other logical model for growth in those countries which spoke different languages, had different cultures and different laws and financial systems. In many countries that they wanted to expand into, a local had to own the business.

"We'll just have to be smarter than we have been," he said. *"What have we learned that we can't repeat?"*

Well, for a start, the last thing Clyde would allow was franchisees ringing him or emailing with problems. That would be someone else's hassle. And Ihe had just the man in mind. Peter, the accountant, was now enjoying his rapid growth and relished having a substantial business. He could handle more. Clyde bought him lunch and offered him a bigger role as Head of Franchising. He took it.

An old lawyer mate drew up the draft franchise contract based on the training franchise model, and Annie and Clyde thought up a growth plan over drinks.

"I like Ramesh," said Annie. *"Why don't we test the market in India?"*

The perfect starting point for the first franchise. India!

They poured another glass and went for a swim.

Now, you're possibly thinking that Clyde and Annie were not strategically methodical. When they had been a small training franchise, they were doing very well, with a turnover of $5m a year, but they wanted more. One of their consultants had been born in America and her mother still lived in Los Angeles. Annie and Clyde had flown to New York and on the way home stopped overnight in LA. Annie bought a copy of the LA Times Saturday Edition, a hugely cumbersome tome that she thought our American consultant might enjoy reading. She did, so much so that she announced she would like to go home to LA. Bloody hell!

So they made the incredibly opportunistic decision to open up in the USA! They made the call because they would otherwise have lost a good consultant, but they decided they would need some comprehensive research. Clyde went online and discovered that California had a population of 22 million. Sydney was a city of only 5 million, and they had grown a $5m business there, so naive logic would suggest that they could have a franchise at least four times bigger in Los Angeles. Enough research! That simplistic deduction led to their pokey overseas office in the City of Angels (an office which lasted only 18 months because while LA may be big, all the head offices are on the other coast of the USA. They could have checked that fact if they'd invested a bit more time.)

But not all business decisions are strategically brilliant. Some feel right but are wrong, others feel wrong but are right and most fall somewhere between. The key is to make the decision when you have minimised the risk.

Clyde decided to use the franchise model to extend the coffee lovers business into non-English-speaking countries. And India would be first if Ramesh agreed. There would be issues but they would deal with them.

They flew first class to the Maldives and after a week, on to Mumbai. Ramesh joined them for dinner at one of Mumbai's finest restaurants and after an indescribable meal, Clyde started speaking: *"Ramesh,"* he said. *"I have a proposition for you. I'd like you to become the world's first franchisee of the ISOCC. For you, we've chosen all of India."*

He then explained that Ramesh would own the rights to the ISOCC Recognition program in India. (Recognition program sounds much more professional than Certificate program, something else that Clyde had picked up as a publicist and spin doctor).

Ramesh sat back in his chair and appeared to mull over the idea. They could see the cogs turning as he added up the figures. Then he stood up, grinned hugely, stepped forward and held out his hand.

"Annie and Clyde. I am honoured beyond honour. How much will this cost?"

"For you, Ramesh, there is no purchase cost, only the percentage of revenue received and I would like you to have one of your people train other franchisees," Clyde said.

What a wonderful and memorable thing to be able to do, to reward someone who has done the right thing by you. You can bury yourself in your day-to-day but times like these need to be cherished.

And so the ISOCC launched its first franchise. India had who knows how many thousands of coffee lounges, road-side coffee bars, restaurants that Ramesh would approach through his team. He would sell certificates at an appropriate price, and the ISOCC would have access to another 1.2 billion potential coffee drinkers.

But while India represented massive potential, Ramesh's best work was still to be delivered to the rest of the world.

CHAPTER FIFTEEN: Then the World!

His team went on-line looking for financial, franchising and marketing/sales magazines and websites. Clyde contacted an old colleague in media placement. They ran the same very small - in fact, single-column - advertisement in each publication, looking for people who wanted to start their own small business from home. Having English, at least as a second language, was preferred.

When they enquired, and hundreds did - Clyde sent them a beautifully-bound (Apple Books $29) comprehensive outline about the world's most successful Coffee Connoisseurs' Society and the opportunity it posed for franchisees.

He was back to doing manual work, but not for long. Clyde shortened the list over the next month and rang a former business partner in his training company. Dave could sell anything to anyone, so Clyde asked him to update his passport. He and accountant Peter left to fly around the world, signing up franchisees. Two days in each country, a PowerPoint presentation and a contract signing where possible. The franchisees had to speak English and needed to have some specific qualities.

Most importantly Dave and Peter rejected those who seemed out for a quick buck, or worse, those who looked like they had aspirations of earning millions. Both groups had proven difficult in the past. The ISOCC needed hard-working, perhaps husband and wife, business people who would not become greedy - even when they became rich beyond their dreams.

Franchising is a sound business model, said Clyde, if your expectations are realistic, but you have to understand that two entities share your profits, the franchisor, and you the franchisee. If the profit is only 20percent on turnover and you pay 15percent to the franchisor, then you only make 5percent. If you start a business from the ground up, then you make the entire 20percent. That division of profits demotivates franchisees when times are tough. While they think the licence fee is fair at the beginning, it seems less fair over time. *"I'm doing all the work, and getting less,"* becomes the catch cry.

The offer read well, with the backing of one of the most comprehensive websites and a track-record of media coverage and membership second to none - in the coffee business anyway. When ISOCC franchisees paid $10,000 upfront, Clyde sent them the How To Do It manual and gave them access to Ramesh, who had his senior trainer run TTT programs in Mumbai.

The How-To-Do-It manual was a combination of the previous works and gave a step-by-step process that anyone could follow.

It's another great lesson. No Intellectual Property is going to be worth much until you write it down and allow others to use it to make money for you. It's about leverage. For example, if you had a brilliant business skills program and you set out to train people in groups of eight, your income would be limited entirely to the time you had available. But if you wrote down how you taught it and then gave others the manual and a few lessons, you could have hundreds of people around the world generating income for you. Clyde had proven it in the past. Leveragability.

Of course, it's essential to establish copyright on your written manuals, because that at least dissuades the cheats for a short while. It will never stop them copying or worse. Clyde had learned the hard way having once hired a training consultant who he nick-named Sniffy. He left the business under a cloud and a week later began running workshops using photocopies of Clyde's workbook. He didn't even remove the copyright footnote from the bottom of the pages. They went to court and the judge declared he would not stop Sniffy earning a living, but he made him change the workbook and remove the copyright footnote! And that sort of rip-off happened in the days before the internet took off!

Clyde knew that establishing copyright was a simple process. All he'd done (another lesson learned over the years) was to create the copyrighted manual then go to the post office and mail a wrapped and tightly-taped copy to himself by registered mail. And when it arrived, he didn't open it. He put it in a cupboard and left it there. What he had established was proof that it had been written before the date on the registered parcel.

New franchisees paid the ISOCC the $10,000 upfront, plus a (terribly modest) 40percent of the turnover. But they didn't do much, and the margin was comparatively huge. All orders for certificates passed quickly through Clyde, but only so he knew the approximate revenue line. Peter and his growing team received the money, banked it and sent 60 percent of it back to the franchisees, who must have thought they'd been hit on the bum by a rainbow. Peter and Clyde would meet for Chinese food overlooking Manly Beach and would study the figures. When Peter tried to complain about the work-load, Clyde shared advice with him: *"Get someone you trust to do it. I got you."*

Clyde had learned about the pitfalls of franchising when he ran his training business. A franchisee is happy when they dream about what they can possibly make, but when they discover it is actually hard work and that much of the profit goes to the franchisor, the dream becomes the harsh reality. When they are earning good money, they work hard, but they seem to want more. But after a while, they get used to the income and their efforts plateau. That's a generalisation, but not too far from the truth.

The trick here was to give them loads of money and have them do very, very, very little, and control even less. Clyde needed their local knowledge and not much else and as a result, he made it so unbelievably rewarding that they would not dare to risk rocking the boat. The Mumbai Army handled fulfilment, so all the franchisee had to do was to follow the manual and wait to receive their enormous cut. They literally had to find a coffee lounge and local paper in each suburb, in each town and tell Mumbai to send the lounge a certificate and media release. Easy money for what they did. Not only did they accept 60percent of the money for the first certificate, but Clyde gave them 30percent of each renewal. Money for jam.

The ISOCC sold franchises in scores of countries including France, Germany, Holland, Denmark, Spain, Italy, Russia, Ukraine, Scandinavia, and Malaysia. (China paid $100,000 upfront because it is a very big country).

Clyde and Annie were very successful franchisors! Well, actually Peter the accountant was because they'd refused to take on the worry. Clyde paid him 15percent of the net income from the network plus costs. He was very happy. The buck stopped with him and so did a good deal of the income. His growing team of bookkeepers handled the money. He only had one real client and a few smaller clients to make him operate as a real company.

There are two sides to any franchise and if you are running franchisees, it requires communication and lots of it. If you don't talk to your franchisee every week, they feel neglected. If you talk to them too often, they feel you need them too much and want more money. You need to be starting, changing and stopping things, or else they will. Peter wisely began paying Ramesh to handle this communication workload. Clyde supplied the business tips and Ramesh's team sent them out.

In the fourth year, the ISOCC turned over an outlandish $65.7 million and paid $28m in tax after allowing for expenses. Unbelievable! *"Too much tax,"* said Peter, so they started giving money away to their favourite charities. Lots of money, millions in fact.

Clyde had always believed that if you worked hard and were successful you needed to give back to your communities. His old management training business had a foundation called Soul which donated thousands in pro bono time to various charities around the world. It was commercially sensible and more importantly a good thing to do. Clyde was a strong advocate of rich people giving money to charity, after all, how much can you spend?

CHAPTER SIXTEEN: We've Arrived!

It was time to test the value of the database. Clyde had always known the power of mining a database, although he'd never had so many clients before. Customers like to know that they buy from companies that are exciting, where things happen, where famous people go, where there is always something new. That's why having the ability to reach your customers through an up-to-date database can be a huge advantage and a source of ongoing revenue.

Clyde collated many of the promotional ideas he'd used in his publicity days. He called it: *'The ISOCC TOP 52 Coffee Lounge Promotional Ideas'*, sub-titled: *'Your Marketing Department in a Box.'* When a member signed up for the package, they received by email 52 individual marketing concepts. The ISOCC showed them how to write a news release, how to organise a coffee tasting, how to run an incentive scheme (buy five coffees and get the sixth free), how to do a promotion on local radio, even how to run a beauty contest because Clyde knew how to do that.

It also contained advice about what NOT to do. He told them of how his PR company had represented a Pest Control company, and a very smart consultant had decided to direct-mail 2000 managing directors with a clever attention-getter. He wrote a powerful letter to each CEO and enclosed in the envelope a plastic cockroach. Wow! At first glance it was brilliant. Except most CEO's mail was opened by their secretary and a surprise cockroach can be frightening. The calls of anger started within forty-eight hours and culminated in a claim for personal damages when a secretary screamed and fell off her chair on to the wastebasket. It pays to think through the ramifications of PR stunts.

The Top 52 included ideas for creating publicity like the pyramid of champagne glasses, which when filled from the top, overflowed down to the bottom, filling each glass. A novel way to fill everyone's glass at a celebratory event, while creating a news photo.

Clyde shared advice like: If you're planning an event of any kind, find a way to make it newsworthy and that means thinking about what would make a good photo. And he told his coffee lounge-owners to read the papers every day, listen to the radio, watch tv and to think in headlines. Newspaper headlines are the designed to make you read the article, so they push the envelope, stretching the reality enough to make you read on. *"Prime Minister in trouble"* might sound exciting, until you read on to find he had been given a parking ticket. *"Small businesses cannot survive"* sounds required reading until you realise it was a quote from a weird Western Sydney University professor known for his outlandish claims. By thinking in headlines, you will become more persuasive in your own marketing. If you understand what papers regularly publish and how they frame it, you can tailor your own marketing materials to be more interesting.

The tips continued. Tip Number 9: Having someone recognise you and know your name is one of the most important things in life, so remember your customer's name then recognise them by using it every time they come into the lounge. Show them they belong. They're a part of your special world. When things are quiet, chat with them - about them. You are growing permanent customers and enjoying yourself at the same time.

Tip Number 34: Mega-association. If a celebrity lives in your suburb, invite them to your lounge for a free coffee. Then ask if you can get a photograph. Send it to your paper, with a quote about what they are doing. If the celebrity agrees, invite the local newspaper down as well for an interview. Make sure they mention the interview happened in your lounge. A free coffee will help.

Tip Number 46: Turn your lounge into the place to be. Make it exciting. Run contests and free giveaways. Think up stunts.

Tip number 27: Contact all the local clubs in your area and offer their members a discount, three for the price of two, or free cake, or anything that will get into the club's newsletter. You want people to be talking about you.

But it was the next idea that turned the coffee lounge members into megastars. The rule from Clyde's PR days was that a small business needs to rise above the rest and become an industry leader. How? By talking on behalf of the industry. He recommended to each member that they offer a weekly column to their local newspaper or community magazine at no cost. But it would always have a tagline stating that the author of "Coffee Essence" was so and so from such and such coffee lounge.

In the column, they would talk about the World of Coffee, in 200 words. It would cost the papers nothing and would not only generate free publicity to the lounge owner but would establish them as being a leader in their field, in their suburb - because they were speaking on behalf of the coffee industry.

Yes, but how does a coffee lounge owner write a column, when they may not be able to write and do not have enough subject matter?

Well, once they have sold the idea to the media, they can pay the ISOCC just $10 a week for which they would receive a free column each week that they can pass on to the newspaper, with their name as the by-line.

Clyde paid a cadet journalist $250 a column, with materials researched from the web, e.g. *"How to make the perfect latte..." "The history of the coffee bean..." "How coffee gets to you..." "Making your milk creamy."* And if 1000 members sold the idea to their media, the ISOCC would be paid $10,000 per article. A modest markup of $9,750, Clyde thought. Not to be sniffed at.

To launch the ISOCC Marketing Department in a Box, Nigel created more time-saving software, and Mumbai followed up by phone offering the kit at an exclusive, **reduced** rate of $250 (Never forget, everyone likes to know they are getting a deal).

On Ramesh's advice, Clyde had him time the calls for around dinner time because most people are home then. Annoying people turn out to be much more acceptable when you are on the right end of the annoyance and when the members heard the Mumbai Army Member say they were ringing on behalf of the International Society of Coffee Connoisseurs, most calls were received well anyway.

Launching the Top 52, as a marketing strategy was relatively expensive, yet by spending a little money, the ISOCC made more. Each client contacted by email and phone cost $4.95. That left a top-line profit of more than $245 per sale. Plus the columns.

Clyde was a little disappointed when only 16,500 signed up, but it was another $4,042,250 for the sock drawer. Minus around $82,500 in costs. Leveragability. And with the marketing tips offer featured on the website, sales continued to roll in.

The International Society of Coffee Connoisseurs had become a full-blown international organisation, known around the world as being the Home of Coffee Lovers. With time had come credibility. Its website had a must-read blog site on which even the odd film-stars, politicians and celebrities showed their knowledge and sophistication around coffee. Major coffee brands chased us for deals:

"Can we sponsor your site?"

"Never!" Clyde replied, *"But you can advertise if the ad is of interest to coffee lounge owners and coffee lovers and if you provide finished art to Michelle and the fee to the ISOCC."*

And so the ISOCC began running advertisements.

If enough people flock to your website, you will attract advertisers. Clyde began running ads for franchise opportunities, for coffee brands and for anyone who needed to reach small businesses.

It was all extra income, icing on the cake.

Clyde even gave the ISOCC a Mission and Purpose, for the website: "**ISOCC - Recognising the art and science of great coffee**" (It wasn't much, but he didn't give it much brainpower either. Visions, and Missions and Purposes and Values are for building and aligning teams, and he did not have much of a team). In the old days, he would have hired a graphic design house and an advertising agency, but he hadn't needed them so far, and he didn't think he would again, ever.)

Michelle hired a team of copywriters and formed a little company that provided the ISOCC site with constant blogs, tips, ideas, and upgrades as well as generating the odd media release.

The ISOCC was now scrupulously legitimate. Having been a journalist, Clyde did worry about the grammar, but Lesley and her small team read every word and made endless corrections to the copy. Not only was the ISOCC big, it was professional!

Then something extraordinary happened. The business began to run out of clients. The Mumbai Marketing Department had been fulfilling beyond anyone's imagination. It could not find anymore online phone directories. Ramesh could see the writing on the wall, even from India. His franchise was going superbly, with more than 23,000 cafes, restaurants and coffee bars under certification, but his team found it hard to keep growing outside India.

Was it time to relax and enjoy the proceeds? Yes, Clyde could survive very comfortably for years on the millions of annual repeat business, but it would gradually and inevitably shrink. Damn it, you grow or you shrink... the only two options.

A step-change was needed, and it was a move that he'd been planning, **and dreading**, for years.

Time for another coffee and a think.

CHAPTER SEVENTEEN:
Understanding the Essence

Clyde had said that there had been two ways he could grow exponentially, the first was to go international and he had done that superbly.

But the second opportunity was stratospherically bigger, and it came from really understanding what the ISOCC was really doing.

The International Society of Coffee Connoisseurs had been taken to the limit, but an absolute truth in business is that you need to understand exactly what it is that you offer your clients, from the clients' point of view. In this case, many could be forgiven for thinking Clyde was in the business of issuing certificates and press releases, but what was the ultimate benefit of what the ISOCC did? What had he really created? From one coffee lounge in Barbados, he'd built an international business for coffee shop owners, but what caused them to keep buying certificates?

What was the ESSENCE of the ISOCC? In reality, they'd built something far more exciting than a certificate business: they'd created a multi-million-dollar 'recognition' business model and a multi-national, franchise and direct business that provided small businesses with their own public relations arm, at minimal cost. It was unique and so successful it had literally saturated the coffee lounge market globally. Its essence lay in that word 'recognition'.

Why not leverage it some more?

The next step was one that was almost too big to think about and was based on just five words: Why limit this concept to coffee?

Clyde had a business model built around helping small business, not just coffee lounge owners. Wouldn't other small businesses like some recognition? Wouldn't every small business owner benefit from a competitive advantage? How unfair it would be if it were only coffee lounges that got marketing help!

Clyde climbed into his new red Jaguar XJR (supercharged) and drove down to the local mall for a latte.

He bought his takeaway coffee at the Gloria Jeans Cafe and commented positively to the owner about her certificate. *"What a tribute to you,"* he gushed. *"You must be pretty proud!"*

"We try hard," she replied.

"What's the International Society of Coffee Connoisseurs?" he asked innocently.

"It's the world's premium body for judging the best coffee," she said. *"It's huge."*

Clyde grinned and took his caramel latte for a stroll.

And this time he did not look for coffee lounges; he looked for shop owners who wanted recognition.

By changing his paradigm from coffee to retailing generally, he saw in that mall a world of opportunities for a proven small business assistance model.

- Was it time for the International Society of Liquor Connoisseurs? People loved booze and bottle shop owners would benefit from being recognised as experts.

- What about hotels? Who wouldn't like their local bar to be recognised globally?

- Seafood Connoisseurs? Which fish shop does not pride itself on the freshest, tastiest seafood?

- The International Society of Health Food Connoisseurs? Health food was 90percent bullshit anyway, I thought. Why not add a bit more through recognition?

- Bread Connoisseurs? Great baking creates fanatics.

- The International Society of Meat-lovers? Highly competitive, butchers need regular happy clientele, who would feel even more comfortable if their butcher had a certificate. An international one.

- Hairdressing Connoisseurs? Hah! Obvious.

Clyde realised that if done well, there was no end. He was making millions from coffee, but obviously, he wasn't thinking BIG enough. First coffee, then the world! Pharmacies? Juice Bars? Stationery shops? Curry shops? Shoe repairers?

Who was he to deprive these fine small businesspersons of their right to a competitive edge?

By understanding the essence of what the ISOCC offered: recognition for small business, he could expand in a hundred new ways, a thousand perhaps.

He had a business model and now he had scope, way beyond the original concept.

CHAPTER EIGHTEEN:
Exponential Growth

Annie was dozing in a deckchair when Clyde shook her awake.

"Annie, Annie!"

"Whaaat?"

"I have an idea. It's eff-ing unbelievable! It's just so BIG I can't get my head around it. We're going to make the business 50 times bigger!!!!"

"Oh shit," she sighed and flopped back down.

Clyde had his solicitor start another twenty-seven International Connoisseur Societies. And warned him that was just the beginning.

He sent his How to Do It manual to a dear friend Bruce, another former partner in the management training business and paid him to tailor the How-To-Do-It coffee manual for 27 different small business groups and he briefed accountant Peter about the next stage. Clyde left him stunned and shaking, and Annie and he flew to Mumbai, via the Four Seasons Resort in Chiang Mai, to find more people.

To Clyde, it seemed like the right thing to do. Leveragability allows exponential growth. If you have a proven business model, you need only to replicate it with minor adjustments. It costs money, but he had lots of that.

He used the same family and friends to form each society and this time paid them $10,000 each to sign the documents. There was nothing that he'd read that prevented someone from being a member of 28 societies. They were just enthusiasts. Daughter Melinda even designed a business card, stating *"Society Creator"* as her job descriptor. She gave a bundle to husband Phil, daughter Tayla and to Kirsty and Brent and their children, Charlie and Summer. *"We are Society Creators,"* she told them.

Clyde budgeted to create one new Society a week for the first month or two, then planned an exponential ramping up. That meant more than 50 Societies in the first year.

When each was formed, he opened a new bank account. Ivan the Banker sought a meeting.

"Clyde, you keep opening more accounts. Our Regional Manager has asked me to find out a bit more about your business. Would that be OK?"

"Sure Ivan," Clyde replied magnanimously. *"What would you like to know?"*

"Well, what do you actually do?"

"We are an international marketing agency for small businesses," I said, trying out my latest barbecue statement. *"We help small businesses everywhere gain the recognition they deserve through publicity and self-promotion. We are the low-cost option for any small business that needs marketing advice and cannot afford to pay the bigger agencies."*

Ivan wrote furiously, ignoring his can of VB.

"Sooo," he said thoughtfully, *"Small businesses pay you for promotional help? But they pay you only $200 a year?"*

"Yes Ivan, but there are a lot of them."

"How many?"

"That's commercially confidential, mate, but there are plenty."

"That seems pretty straightforward," he confided. *"I have to tell you, I don't know a lot about most of my customers' businesses but yours seems very simple and very successful."*

"Another beer, mate?"

Clyde had found it hard to get his head around the bigger concept, and it **was** very complex if everything had to be done at once. But what he was doing, he reminded himself, was using the coffee mould to punch out identical models. And the first big realisation was that he could replicate everybody else not himself. There was no way he could do more. He took a piece of paper and drew a triangle on it with himself at the top. Then he put a dotted line straight down from himself to a CEO, and from that box down to 10 more, then from each of them to 10-12 more.

He decided sixty would be the number of Society managers he'd need to service his planned societies.

Now he had to find a business model that worked like that. He needed 60 Society GM's with managers above them and then someone else to actually run the lot, leaving him free to "create".

Those 60 Society managers had to be capable and serious business folk who would follow a manual to the letter, who could work hard and who understood people; who took orders well and understood they were a part of a bigger business. They needed rigour and discipline.

And he knew just where to find them because he'd met lots of them when he was in PR.

Supermarkets!

Woolworths, for example, was a $60 billion business in Australia alone, comprised of 1500 stores each turning over millions per year and run by store managers who followed the

Woolworths manual to the letter. That was the skill set that he needed. He would get himself 28 Woolworths or Coles or IGA or Aldi managers by writing to 500 of them at their stores and interviewing 100. Each already earned a good salary, but not compared to his offer, which included a lot fewer hours per week and a 10 percent share of the income each new certificate issued.

He hired first 15 then 30 and, as the word spread, 60 Society General Managers. As store managers, each had spent their working lives appreciating that every dollar counted, that every customer was a person who needed looking after, that reporting was essential and that there was only ONE way to run a business: The Company Way. And each was interchangeable, so if a Society failed, they could move into another.

Clyde gave them a two-month-long tutorial, a boot camp in which the Train the Trainer manuals were God. They relished the training because they had lived in an organisation that believed in training. They flew to Mumbai and they met Peter and Nigel, Lesley and Michelle. And as they graduated Clyde had them work with an existing Society GM to learn the ropes.

He robbed Woolies and Coles again for Regional managers, who had all been store managers and had the same rigour in what they did. He had those "Group Society" general managers each control ten or more Society Managers. The five Group managers reported to the MD of Societies who was a GM from Coles Head Office. Penny knew all about replication and reporting and turning tiny profit margins into millions.

She reported to Clyde, but only occasionally.

Nigel's fishing days were behind him, for a while anyway. His IT company flourished as he kept minimising the business's human input and maximising IT. What had worked with the ISOCC worked with each new Society. When it needed people to ring up and do the manual work, Ramesh provided.

Within six months, Stage Three of the Global Expansion Strategy was well and truly underway. Clyde hadn't underestimated for a second how much more complex it would become because he was taking a $50 million-plus business and replicating it over and over again. But by appointed supermarket GM's he was using managers who knew how to run tight ships. His managers had been part of multi-billion-dollar businesses, so this little ship was relatively small by comparison.

Ramesh cloned his original team into 20 more groups, using the experienced coffee people to train new employees and using the manuals to ensure accuracy.

But would the coffee model work for other small businesses?

They set off to find out.

First was The Society of World's Leading Publicans. Note the details in the name: "Society" to keep the credibility, "World's Leading" because this is all about recognition and ego; "Publicans" because every pub is defined by the personality of the publican and, cynically, they control the budgets.

Clyde created the first certificate for his son-in-law's pub in Bowral. The Imperial Hotel's publican Brent was named the Best Publican in Bowral, Southern Highlands. He put it on the wall next to his coffee certificate, but not near his wife Kirsty's Best Pub Restaurant certificate.

The SOWLP took off as Clyde thought it would. He seeded pubs in the suburbs of 28 cities using exactly identical techniques to those perfected in coffee. Surprised publicans found they had been nominated to join the ranks of the world's leading publicans. As expected there was a flow of enquiries about certificates and stories. Then Clyde unleashed the Mumbai Mob, and like a self-fulfilling prophecy, the Society grew.

As it took off, Clyde launched others. He was able to move more quickly now. He'd a rapidly-expanding web team who ignored the coffee site for a while and filled the pub site with stories of the world's oldest, smallest, largest, quaintest pubs. Facebook and LinkedIn followed. Personality stories ran everywhere.

Within weeks, pub chains tried to buy certificates in bulk and were told that the SWLP only dealt with individual hotels. Would they care to send us a list of their hotels?

Lesley had set up a proofreading team, hired a general manager and retired to her beach house. As she said: *"Proofreading is deadly accurate, but not complex. Others can do it."*

Peter's accountancy practice had grown into a sizeable outfit, merging with a slightly bigger company and taking naming rights on a building in the CBD. He'd come a long way from two rooms in Manly.

A week after the pub program, Clyde launched The International Society of Health Food Retailers, and a week later The World Bakery Lovers Society and the Global Wine Appreciation Association and, over the next year, 22 more. He was insatiable for Societies and kept forming and building, replicating the simple model.

Another massive learning for Clyde: Each Society only existed online and discreetly to its members. The web is a huge place filled with trillions of pieces of information, so being able to exist separately was not the issue it could have been. And best of all, nobody need ever find that the one person was behind all of the societies. If that ever happened, it could be interesting.

CEO Penny appointed Australia's largest personnel agency and briefed them to hire people in bulk. Programmers for Nigel. Bookkeepers and managers for Peter's franchise business. Bruce and his trainer mates wrote manuals and he bought himself a nice cruiser. Lesley sat in her beach-front holiday house, just feet from the sand, occasionally checking in with her general manager of proofreading. The website writers expanded their company, under the guidance of their Chairman Michelle.

They carried all of the pain involved with running people. Clyde just funded growth.

Over the next three years, the Recognition Business became a very, very, very big, conglomeration of small entities. Clyde had made many millions from coffee and now he was making millions more from every group of companies that dealt with customers.

If he'd thought coffee lounge-owners were going to make him rich, he hadn't considered what would happen when he replicated the business model in hotels, wine-bar owners, health food stores, corner shops, service stations, hairdressers (but not barbers), pharmacies, and fish shops. Jewellers were a gold mine, boutiques, and accountants.

Then there were restaurants - not restaurants in general but specifically Chinese restaurants, Thai, Vietnamese, Greek, Spanish, French. Each needed its own discreet recognition entity, e.g. the International Society of Chinese Cuisine Connoisseurs, the International Society of Greek Cuisine Connoisseurs.

Each new society was successful, but nothing was as easy as it had been when he'd launched the ISOCC. The publicity was now much harder to get and the overheads substantial, but not yet onerous. The new Societies tended not to grow as quickly, but the income from coffee was still joined by an average of $10m per society over five years, multiplied by some 58 societies. The not gigantic business headed by one person who didn't want overheads was approaching $600,000,000 a year and each year each society delivered millions more for nothing, in automatic renewals.

Was it crazy? Yep! Had it been based on nothing but an idea? Yep. Had it turned over $600 million? Yep. From one latte in a cafe called Cassareep. Yep.

Did it have a profit margin of 67.5percent or $405 million? Yep.

But did Clyde have a profile? Nope. Did he want one? Nope.

But he did buy another new computer and upgraded his coffee machine? Yep again.

CHAPTER NINETEEN:
Handling Rough Times!

Clyde didn't know who had first said: *"All good things must come to an end"*. He'd had a few mates who shook their heads when he told them what he was doing, but he'd dismissed their concerns as a lack of understanding. He should have realised that their concerns could be shared by others, millions of others.

Money was not the problem - he had too much of it. He was giving it away to charities, a million at a time, to lower tax and also because he could and should.

His bank accounts were full of after-tax money. He created what an old mate Geoff called a "f...-off fund" by taking bundles of $100,000 and putting them in a large combination safe room under the floor of their new waterfront home (which he had put in Annie's name, just in case). It was after-tax money but who trusted banks really? What if something went wrong? He spent a significant sum on plastic rubbish bags and wrapped each bundle carefully.

He also bought shares through the new trust he'd set up for Annie and the children - only bank shares, but lots of them. He didn't buy gold because he'd have to find a place to keep it and the safe room was filled with cash. And he'd never figured out if you actually buy real gold or the promise of it.

But the money machine simply did not stop turning. Each year the renewals alone generated close to half a billion. Income from investments added to the burden. *"Well, not really a burden,"* Annie said. *"More of a problem that anyone else in the world would kill to have."*

But, there was a niggle starting in Clyde's brain and moving to the gut. Something would go wrong. It couldn't last. Surely it couldn't last. The train was roaring down the track, whistle screaming, belching steam… but there was every chance that there could be a sharp bend ahead.

Perhaps he should sell or float before it all went belly-up?

Joe was a venture capitalist who had made himself very wealthy buying companies and then funding their growth. Years ago, pre-September 11, he'd bought into one of Clyde's businesses then sold out three years later. They had a coffee and discussed what Clyde called *"my little Recognition Business"*.

At first, Joe showed confusion, then shock, then he went white.

"WHAT is it you do?" he said.

"See those certificates on the wall over there?" Clyde said, pointing to the ISOCC diplomas. *"That's what we do."*

"What, you print things?"

"Not really, I get the client to do their own printing," Clyde said. "I help small businesses grow by getting them recognition. *I'm the world's cheapest marketing department."*

"But you only give them a certificate!"

"Yes, and a color one at that," I told him. *" But we do a lot more. We give them publicity, we give them tips on growing their business, we give them a competitive edge. And we do it for next to nothing."*

"You're joking! You're giving them certificates from Societies that don't exist until you start them!"

"You're making it sound bad."

"It is bad. It's impossible!"

"Here are the figures." And Clyde pushed a single sheet of paper over the table. Joe blanched.

"Bugger me, you're either a genius or quite mad," he said, shaking his head. *"But I can't do anything for you. No bank or decent-sized*

company will touch you with a barge pole. It's working, but it's all froth and bubbles!"

They moved on to other topics.

But Joe had summed up what had been nagging Clyde. At first glimpse and even second glance, it still seemed like a scam. A million-dollar rip-off. But that wasn't true and anyone who ran a small business that had been helped by the program knew it. Nor was it any longer true about our Societies, most of which had plenty of members, and decent websites albeit filled with mainly OPS (other people's stuff).

What was difficult to comprehend was that the business model itself could work so well. And each part of it did work beautifully with the others. Because of the certificate, Clyde could get the $200 from many thousands of businesses. Because of the certificate, they got publicity that generated more certificates. Because of the website, the certificates had credibility. Because of the Magnificent Mumbai team, they could generate the emails and the calls needed to keep growing. Because of the franchisees, they could operate in non-English-speaking countries. Because of their training expertise, they could get them up to speed quickly. Everything gelled; each component delivered its own discreet but critical element.

Yet Clyde's experience was that a good idea only lasted as long as it took for others to copy it. They were open for someone else to replicate what they did. Once anyone understood the simple model, idiots could do it with a computer, as Clyde had proven.

And as expected, he started to see one or two new societies forming and awarding certificates.

One of Peter's former employees started up The International Society of Hardware Aficionados, and then the International Association of Automotive Repair Experts. She sold a few certificates around Australia using representatives who visited each hardware store. It went nowhere because her overheads bogged her down. No copyist had the first-mover advantage that the ISOCC team had, none had the enormous clout of their hundreds of thousands of members, the websites, the blogs, the special offers, the coffee championships, the thousands of testimonials from happy recipients who claimed the ISOCC had helped to build their business, the cable TV shows on coffee, baking, and hairdressing. (Clyde had licensed these to avoid overheads and took a royalty on each show).

Nobody had the **brand** in the New World of Recognition.

And quite frankly, Clyde didn't care a great deal about what others did or might do. He'd spent years fretting about competitors and he'd learned that worrying was a hiding to nothing. His philosophy was to go hard and fast and let the others catch up if they could. That first-mover advantage was the key. A strong brand won over price every time. If you don't stand still, they can't catch you.

Sure there were issues, most of which Clyde ignored. But the Tax Department audited the business and gave a clean slate, the lesson being that if you earn enough you can afford to pay all your bills including tax - and you will sleep at night.

Nevertheless, Clyde was getting a little nervous at the sheer volume of members, societies, money flowing towards him.

But he was ready for it to hit the fan. So far he'd been lucky in that nobody had made the link between the ISOCC and the other societies covering different retail sectors. But that would happen. And if it did it could give people the wrong impression. Truth does not necessarily make the most interesting headlines. Clyde knew he had done nothing wrong, but would others agree?

He was more than a little paranoid and yet prepared for the worst, having fought crises and issues for years as a PR man. He'd been taught by a mentor, the late Russell Smith, that when faced with an issue you follow three maxims: You do not fuel the fire; you let your friends do your fighting and you never try to convince those who will never be convinced.

He also had a secret weapon called the 'Spin Doctors'. He'd formed a lunch club in 1994 after Sydney won the rights to stage the Year 2000 Olympic Games. Simon was a minder in the Organising Committee Head Office. Clyde was working in communications for the Games. Sponsors were getting more and more worried that they were being kept in the dark about what was happening, so Simon and Clyde formed the Spin Doctors, to which they invited Richard, Marketing Director of the sponsoring bank, Anthony the Marketing Director of a major shopping centre sponsor, and Adrian the Corporate Affairs Director of the huge mining company sponsor. The simple strategy was to get pissed, really pissed, and tell them the truth about what was really going on the organising committee headquarters. It worked a treat in terms of calming the waters, as open communication tends to do.

When the Games ended in 2000, they had kept the club going, changing a member or too, but sharing a love of communication, spin, crises, and issues. They printed a teeshirt which said: *"Just because you're not paranoid doesn't mean we're not out to get you."* But they were toothless and knew it.

They'd met every single year since, often three times a year.

So Clyde had some weapons when the wheels started to seriously wobble.

And they did.

CHAPTER TWENTY: Dealing with Crises

The first issue was that most shops nowadays seemed to have a certificate on their wall, recognising them for whatever they did. So a stroll through a shopping mall had become a journey of reading endless certificates, many of which looked remarkably similar, despite the best efforts of daughter Melinda. Once you've changed a certificate from portrait to landscape, changed the colors and fiddled with the layout, you eventually run out of options.

Some recipients cancelled their subscriptions because they felt it was no longer exclusive. Clyde couldn't blame them.

The bigger issue was that no suburban newspapers any longer thought the certificate stories worthy of inclusion because there were so many of them. They were so common they were no longer news. So the new businesses were relying almost entirely on direct mail to reach new customers.

Another problem was that by choosing one business in each suburb, the businesses annoyed thousands of others who did not get recognition. Many had tried to and had been given them a certificate if it was not an obvious clash with an existing member, but some businesses were next door and others had mates who had received one. They were not happy. They were envious, and that's a powerful emotion.

Some businesspeople might panic when things start to go pear-shaped, but Clyde didn't. You can over-react to something and by doing so, create a worse situation. So when 23 non-member shop-owners in Melbourne banded together to demand an explanation, Clyde poured a 2011 Hunter Vineyard Cabernet Sauvignon and dropped their letter into the trash bin. Nothing happened because nobody had really been hurt. Everybody had received a certificate and a story and business tips and what's $200 bucks today?

And who do you run to, the local newspaper or radio station? They'd been a part of the promotion, so they would be unlikely to find fault with their involvement.

Ironically, some members who'd cancelled came back when they realised that the certificate had become an expectation of their customers. Coffee drinkers and hotel patrons would say things like: *"What happened to your certificate?"* By not having the certificate, they risked appearing to have had a drop in standards. It was easier to keep renewing them. The certificate had become a ticket to entry, a cost of doing business and a small cost at that.

As a customer, if you didn't drink coffee in a lounge recognised by the ISOCC, you might be getting an inferior experience. The ISOCC certificate was a genuine stamp of approval.

After a client (Clyde now called them clients because it sounded more prestigious) had received a certificate for three consecutive years, Clyde simplified things by announcing that they would automatically be sent one each year. They had proven their consistency and all they had to do was pay the fee each year, through a regular direct debit. The ISOCC guaranteed that the price would not go up and didn't have to keep selling each renewal each year. Hundreds of thousands took up the offer.

Clyde, having worked as a consultant for many public companies in the past, found it enormously refreshing not to have to report to a Stock Exchange. The ridiculous need to keep improving every 90 days so people would invest, was not an issue he faced. If he had a poor result in one quarter, nobody knew. He just shrugged.

Among the clients, there were the few Don Quixotes who decided that something smelled and mounted their Rosinantes to do battle, but most were cranks and their approaches went nowhere. If Clyde had to, he responded to their complaints with a formal letter, reiterating their

Society's legitimacy but adding nothing to fuel the fire. And Peter sent their money back.

It was only $200 bucks anyway and refunding it killed off most complaints because they had a little win.

If Clyde had a major looming problem, it was the tall poppy syndrome. If anyone put it all together, then it would appear simply too successful, too big and too interesting. Even the individual societies were now big enough in their own right to make people wonder about how they worked and who might be behind them. Put together they were a massive news story with a bigger human-interest story behind it.

The Australian media rejoices in cutting down the tallest poppies.

Clyde knew that from the corporate PR days.

His advice to clients had always been: *"Keep your head down. It's not about you, it's about your business. Let others promote you, but never be seen to be seeking publicity yourself. Publicity that helps your company achieve its goals is worth seeking, but publicity about how good **you** are, only feeds an ego, your ego. If you become a personality, the media will build you up, but they will cut you down when you trip. So stay humble!"*

It had always been sound advice and he intended to follow it.

Until now the press had only been annoying in that they occasionally tried to find and interview the people behind the Societies. Not that there were any. The Society managers were not allowed to use their names in the business. Clyde hadn't used his name since Cassareep's certificate. They couldn't track down Chairman Gerry, and if they did he would tell them straight-faced that he was a titular head and had lent his name only. Sure he might get a bit cranky because of all the attention, but his wife Martha loved the 2013 Hunter Vineyard Gewurztraminer, boxes of which arrived regularly in a small van. Clyde told him he was not at all titular but certainly a bit of a tit for having had him fired.

Clyde was a recluse as far as the media was concerned. Nobody even knew he was behind it. No media enquiry received more than a standard snub. It's a terrible example, he thought, but in that way, we're like Scientology, without all the brainwashing.

"International man of mystery," daughter Kirsty said.

The waterfront home was a fortress. And the businesses kept growing. Clyde still really only dealt with three or four people, usually by phone or over coffee. They, of course, dealt with many more, but never the media. Peter's firm had no obvious link nor did Nigel's IT business. All employees signed confidentiality agreements on their hiring.

It should have been enough, but you never know in a world where information flows so openly.

And after years of media niggles, things suddenly got serious.

The Daily Herald, ironically a newspaper where Clyde had worked as boating editor all those years ago had been approached by two north shore housewives with an amazing story about their having been employed to create hundreds of certificates for coffee lounges. They gave an exclusive about how they'd churned out certificates unceasingly for a strange man (how dare they!) who lived nearby. "It was a sham, a con," they stated with all the hypocrisy of people who were once doing very well, then got greedy, then felt slighted.

Clyde kicked himself again for not having handled their dismissal in a more generous way; for letting his initial frustration lead to the wrong decision. It could have been an elegant solution; instead, it had been a bit brutal. What had been a tiny matter then was now going to create pain.

Two of the paper's investigative journalists began to dig. They sought an interview through the ISOCC website and did not get a helpful response. 'It is Society policy not to grant interviews,' The ISOCC stated. The journalists still had no names and telephone numbers. But they dug deeper and discovered no less than 113 coffee lounges in Sydney, that were displaying certificates.

"Did you know this was a con?" they asked each owner. (This is known as the leading question and it works well when dealing with those who are media ignorant.)

"No, of course not," they said. (If Clyde had trained them they wouldn't have accepted the premise in the question. They would have said: *"**You** have called it a con. I did not."*)

Clyde knew that if reporters got one person to corroborate a story that would be enough to make it worth running. If they got 10, that would serve as virtually irrefutable proof. But if they got 113, God couldn't convince them of their error.

Years of coaching leaders in dealing with the media had shown him that proof was not always truth. The definition of proof, from Clyde's training program, had always been: *'The right amount of the right kind of evidence needed to convince the decision-maker."* It didn't have to be true, just convincing enough. The Herald journalists were collecting a huge amount of the right kind of evidence namely *'poor deceived little shop owners'* and it appeared damning to the readers who knew nothing about what the ISOCC had really done for its clients.

The first story ran on page three with two bylines. If Clyde had been the complainants' publicist, he'd have been delighted. It told of a scam to swindle hundreds of small business owners.

By Day Two it had grown to fill most of a page, with another 202 coffee lounges coming forward, most to add their names to the list of the aggrieved. It was becoming a *'multi-million-dollar scam'*.

National Radio picked it up briefly and dropped it.

Thankfully, most other media didn't go with it, because the Herald had an exclusive and wouldn't share its sources. That's another good lesson. If a media outlet has sources, it will protect them so other media cannot get access to the roots of the story. But it means the story is harder to grow into something spectacular because the other media don't have it. Still, the Herald felt it was on a good thing and it kept riding forth to save the world. Shock! Horror! Scandal!

Then on Day Five, when the paper started to run out of new angles, another newspaper published the astounding claim from a fruit shop owner that she also had a certificate, and so did her brother the butcher and her hairdresser and her bottle shop and local pub. This was no longer a story about coffee certificates - the genie was out of the bottle.

Online searches by journalists quickly revealed that the *'certificate scam'* was, in fact, multi-faceted and global. Within a week there were stories in London, New York, LA, Auckland, Singapore, and Johannesburg.

The Herald claimed it was the *'Rort of the Century'*.

Clyde's Society inboxes exploded with mail. *"What is happening? Is this a con game? How dare you!"*

The Society's started getting thousands of negative blogs on all of the 58 websites and these added fuel to the fire. Facebook turned ugly. The rest of social media went mad with interest.

Gerry phoned from Budapest after reading a story in The Daily Hungary, the English paper in his city.

"In a bit of strife, mate?"

"Perhaps, but I don't think so," Clyde replied.

"Perhaps you should have stayed retired."

"What and miss out on all this?"

"We've really enjoyed the dinners. Can I help in any way?"

"Can I borrow a few trucks for my money?"

"Ha ha."

CHAPTER TWENTY-ONE:
Keep Smiling!

Could it get any worse? Well, they still didn't have Clyde's name, did they?

Of course, he'd spoken too soon. The reporters were given a tip. An Australian tourist visiting Barbados had seen a certificate on the wall of little café in Speightstown, and it had been signed by a "Clyde West" as CEO and Gerry Burke as Chairman. Ooops!

Now they had something to get their teeth in to. An online search of the Government websites found that Clyde's name and those of his family were involved in 58 societies in total, all formed in the past five years. Worse, they found the same signatories made up the original Society members of every single association.

Clyde's family threw away their business cards.

The media tried desperately to contact him and failed. But quite a few people, not necessarily friends but former employees and others who had known him came forward to talk to the media. Not all were kind.

"He tried to sue me when I left his business."

"He used to be a reporter, a pretty crook one."

"I was an entrant in a beauty contest he ran. It was rigged."

Peter's business was approached, but he didn't say anything, citing client confidentiality.

Nigel and Bruce went fishing.

But by not responding Clyde was creating a media vacuum, one that would be filled by supposition and assumption and by those who claimed to know what was going on, but didn't. Clyde had taught clients that if you don't become the source of the facts, others will fill that vacuum, to your detriment.

And then, of course, there was the inevitable ambulance-chasing lawyer who announced that she was launching a multi-million-dollar class action on behalf of all those 'duped'. She called for people to sign up to sue the people behind this scheme.

Meanwhile, Clyde poured Annie a Peroni and opened a vintage Moet et Chandon. They sat and watched the ferries plying across Sydney Harbor as the waves lapped their jetty.

Annie kept asking questions:

"Who's suffered?" (Clyde couldn't think of anybody who had not done well out of it).

"Who didn't get what they paid for?" (Nobody).

"Who's out of pocket?" (Certainly not us).

"Who's not better off?" (Well, certainly, we are, but so are all the clients, who each gained recognition and publicity at low cost).

Clyde considered and applied the Eight Rules of Crisis Management that ironically he had helped create and had taught to businesspeople, starting with Russell Hill's three:

1. **Don't Fuel the Fire** means if the decision is made to comment publicly on the issue, don't make it worse by giving your detractors more fuel. The ISOCC had not commented in any way that would make things worse. If Clyde went public, that could well make things really interesting. But there comes a time when you have to correct inaccuracies if you can do so without adding wood to the pyre. It might be time to go public. There was the matter of principle!

2. **Let your friends do the fighting** means sometimes it's better to say nothing and have others (end users, suppliers, clients, partners, valued friends) speak on your behalf. Clyde had, he was certain, many thousands of small business owners who had received real value for their money. How could he mobilise them to do the fighting? Park that thought.

3. **Don't waste time trying to convince those who will never change their minds** means make sure you are not wasting your resources on those who will never listen or change. Clyde was sure there were those who would always think it was a scam, but the key was to ring-fence their influence. He had to find a way to shut them down while talking to those who would listen to reason.

4. **Protect your values** means make sure your actions are seen as being consistent with your company values and with the expectations of your stakeholders. Interesting indeed! The ISOCC and the other Society's too had always delivered value from the first certificate in Cassareep. They had never ripped people off. They had in fact added value to those who needed it most. They were the 'virtual marketing department' for thousands of tiny businesses. And they were also small bikkies when it came to individual sums of money. Any response would have to be small in scope, reflecting the ISOCC's unsophisticated nature.

5. **Stay in Control** means check that you are not reacting to someone else's lead. Is there a better time to act? Who's starting, changing and stopping things? How do we get on to the front foot? This was even more fascinating. Clyde certainly refused to be chased down the road by television cameras, clambering through gardens

to escape, holding his hand up over the lens and swearing. (although he'd helped clients who had done that). So going public might be an issue, at this time. Park that for later too.

6. **The paranoia check** means you need to come to a decision as to whether you're being paranoid, or not paranoid enough. Is this an over-reaction? Is there another agenda behind this issue? Who is benefiting? Clyde wondered how long the 'scandal' would really last. Who cared in the end? Who sweated over $200? Collectively it was hundreds of millions, but individuals only ever paid a tiny sum. Based on that, realistically how long would it last?

7. **Prepare for a reaction** means making sure that in taking any decision, you've prepared for the reaction. E.g., if the phones start to ring will our employees know what to say? Well, Clyde's phone was not going to start ringing, because only a handful of people had the number. He had no employees and only had one unlisted number which he would get rid of if it rang. He'd told everyone involved to shut up.

8. **Beyond the Lawyers** means seek legal input early but also ask: "If we weren't liable legally, how might we act? What's the right thing to do?" Owning up now to something that is a 'little wrong' is always better than covering

it up and having to explain that particular decision later. Another one to park for a while.

Clyde called a meeting of the Spin Doctors Lunch Club and after our fourth bottle of Pinot Grigio, he posed a hypothetical.

He told them that he was very close to the situation they had read about in the Herald and he laid it out, detail by detail. He then called for suggestions on how they might help this 'client.'

And help they did, albeit only until the alcohol turned sound advice to wild, uproarious laughter, made worse by his admitting that the 'client' was himself.

But they did have opinions, blurry opinions:

Adrian: "Stay below the radar."

Richard: "Go public"

Anthony: "Sell. What is it you do again?"

And then later…

Adrian: "Run for your f-ing life!"

Anthony: "Where's my certificate you stingy bastard?"

Simon: "Bribe them."

Adrian: "Put a hit on them"

John: "More wine!"

Richard: "Ya know Clyde... I've always admired you. No really, I have. I really, really, REALLY admire you, Clyde. But I think you're rooted."

And so it continued, bottle by bottle, Lemincello after Pear William. Perhaps Clyde had better do it himself.

This much he knew. If he hired lawyers, it would be a costly and endless procedure. But it might be an idea to get one opinion.

Graham was retired now, traveling a bit and dining out a lot. He'd been Clyde's lawyer for twenty years and valued not for his Rottweiler attitude but for his common sense. Clyde had dinner and talked him through it. He laughed so hard and so loudly they were asked to leave the restaurant and he was still giggling when they moved to a bench on the beach.

Clyde asked him about the pending legal action.

"Good luck to her with a class action," he roared. *"For a start, the most anyone could claim is probably between $200 and $600. And anyone who joins the action will have to contribute to the lawyer's fees. Worse for the lawyer, everyone has received exactly what they paid for!"*

Ironically Clyde could be safe because he didn't charge enough?

He asked Graham what he'd done wrong legally.

"Well, probably nothing," he said. *"You started very small societies and then built them. But that's not your problem. Your problem is that you can win the rational fight, but you might lose the emotional one. This is a fight that is being fought in the media, not in the courts."*

He was right.

Later that night at home, Clyde went to the fridge and found Annie her beer and put an idea to her. She nodded and he rang Nigel and Peter and sent an email to Mumbai. Peter, Nigel, and Ramesh went to work.

When you're under attack, he thought, you either keep your head down and pray it will go away, or you go on to the attack.

This was becoming a matter of principle, and worse, it had legs of its own and was running very, very quickly.

CHAPTER TWENTY-TWO:
When you become famous

The media scrimmage continued for days with journalists knocking themselves out trying to reach Clyde and when failing, speaking to those who had known him.

"Certificate Man once ran Miss Boat Show Quest!"

"I fired Certificate Man!"

"I smelled a rat," says **coffee lounge owner."**

"Certificate Man ran Bellyflop Championships!

"Weird history of Certificate Man."

"The award-winning coffee was disgusting."

"Budapest link to Certificate Man."

"Small businesses challenge certificate selections."

"I was robbed", **says Bill the Butcher.**

"Best presentation coach I ever had," **says Reserve Bank Governor.**

"He poached my managers," **says supermarket chief.**

Gerry was approached in Budapest by the European correspondent for one of the TV channels. *"Piss off,"* he told the journalist, giving the finger to the camera. It looked superb on Sydney TV the next night.

Clyde congratulated him on his superior communication skills.

"Thanks, mate," he said. *"I should have been the trainer, not you."*

Meanwhile, our intrepid Herald journalists were seeking ways to keep breathing life into the story. They approached the Premier of the State and asked what the Department of Fair Trading was going to go about it, asking, *"Why didn't you know? How did you allow this to happen?"*

The Minister for Fair Trading announced that an investigation was being launched and that no further comment would be made until that investigation was concluded.

The headline read: *"Fair Trading Minister launches investigation into Global Certificate Scam"*.

But nobody from Government rang Clyde.

Ironically, it was one columnist's contribution in the Australian, that had finally goaded him into action. She wrote a thoughtful piece in which she argued that nobody had really suffered and many businesses had won. But she added: *"In the end, this matter boils down to that of ethics and that, in turn, will be decided by the answer to the question: 'What came first the chicken or the egg?' If Mr. West issued certificates before any Society existed then that was unethical. However, if the Societies were formed first then they could have legitimately given the certificates."*

It was certainly time to press a button. And Clyde did.

On the following Wednesday, every single website – 58 of them – shut down, replaced by a single statement. Simultaneously, Ramesh sent out an email to every member of every society in every English-speaking country around the world in which Clyde had businesses. The franchisees translated it and emailed their own members.

Clyde had written it as if he was talking to each individual member, something that some politicians and even newsreaders forget: That we listen and watch as individuals, therefore they should always talk to us as individuals. That means they should not say: *"Good evening everyone"* because the use of the word *"everyone"* proves you are not talking to me. Instead, they should talk as if speaking one-to-one. You say, not *"Good evening everybody,"* but just *"Good evening."* It's more powerful because each person reading your letter, or hearing you speak in public feels you are talking to them alone. So Clyde's email was personalised:

"Dear Personal name,

It is with a very sorry heart I have to inform you that the International Society of XXXXXXXXX is no more. Due to malicious and misleading media, we have decided to cease to trade. Because of this, we can therefore no longer offer our marketing services to the thousands of small businesses like yourself, who have relied on us for so many years. Since inception, this Society has sought only to help small business persons like yourself, assisting with your marketing and giving you the recognition that you and your family so richly deserve. As it has grown, it has become a home for those devoted to your profession and has brought many hours of reading pleasure, business advice and shared experience to thousands of members. Unfortunately, elements of the media have decided that erroneous tabloid headlines are more important.

The following services have been cancelled:

- *No more certificates will be issued recognising superlative performance of small businesses, including your own.*

- *Consequently, you will need to arrange your own local publicity. However, we strongly recommend you do not create a certificate yourself because you do not have the backing of an international society.*

- *Over the past years, we have provided you with marketing tips to help you build your business. These will now be discontinued, due solely to the efforts of so-called investigative journalists.*

- *There will be no more stories on the subject about which you are most passionate.*

- *Our website is no more and with it the blogs to which you contributed so well and so often. We apologise that you will have to find other means to share ideas with fellow devotees.*

- *The total cost for our core services has been a very cost-effective $200 a year, but only for those who have been awarded the color certificate. That equates to 55 cents per day for a range of services.*

- *We hope you continue the relationship we helped you establish with your local media and trust you now understand better how to promote your business.*

- *During the course of our relationship, we have been able to support many charities* *around the world, to a total of $8.35 million, a hugely-positive move, which most unfortunately, we will now have to discontinue. However, I'm delighted to be able to advise you that today we have made a final donation, on your behalf and on behalf of all the members around the world, a further sum of $10 million dollars to the Happiness Children Foundation, to provide a total of 15,000 wishes to be granted for children who are seriously and terminally ill. This has been made possible because of your support and is the largest donation ever received by that worthy charity. On the children's behalf and on behalf of their families we thank you.*

• *We believe that small business owners like yourself have been ignored for years, over-taxed, dragged down with red tape and given little or no support. We have seen our role as being to try to help you prosper.*

"Should you wish to express your opinion about what has occurred, and wish to speak up on behalf of small businesses everywhere, please feel free to ring or write to The Editor, Daily Herald Editor@dailyherald.com.au You should also email Nick Verter c/o the Herald nickV@dailyherald.com.au and Harry Winstone also with the Herald. HarryW@dailyherald.com.au.

Ramesh and his team not only hit the phones but contracted fellow telemarketers in Mumbai, contacting as many members as possible by phone at dinner time, of course.

Their message was one of apology about the end of the service, with a request for the listener to contact their local media and their local Member of Parliament.

The same message appeared on Facebook and LinkedIn.

But more was needed than the attack through social media, direct email and telephoned.

Clyde prepared a statutory declaration and had it sworn by a Justice of The Peace. It was a clarification statement of some 20 pages, simply telling the story of Cassareep. It added nothing except irrefutable facts. There was no emotion. It did not fuel the fire. It gave dates and times and included his favorite photograph of himself, head and shoulders, leaning slightly forward, looking younger, because it had been taken 15 years earlier. (Another PR trick that always works).

And he sent it to AAP Reuters and through Media Monitors to every media outlet that wanted it.

It began:

A STATEMENT FROM Clyde West

"Five years ago, in Barbados, a friend and I helped a young struggling coffee lounge-owner, Sam Golesorkhi, with the promotion of his coffee lounge by presenting him with a certificate commending the quality of his coffee. We did not charge. It was done in good faith, in a manner that hurt nobody and helped a small businessman. The first meeting of the International Society of Coffee Connoisseurs had occurred 24 hours before the issue of the first free certificate. A dear friend Gerry Brooke and I had realised that there was a place for a Society dedicated to aficionados of fine coffee and we shook hands in an agreement to form the International Society of Coffee Connoisseurs. At that point, the Society was underway.

On returning to Australia I began the formal stage of the formation of the Association.

I formed the Society with members of my family and began issuing certificates of appreciation to those coffee lounges that we thought worthy of recognition. Because there was a fast-growing demand it became too expensive to continue the service pro bono and I added a small charge, unchanged today. This annual fee, which equates to just 55 cents per day per year per small business, covered servicing costs and design work involved in not only providing a certificate for each chosen lounge, but also *delivering continual professional marketing assistance by way of a media release for their local newspapers, a major website and ongoing tips on marketing. At no time was the charge made without the explicit approval of and at the request of the business in question. In the very few cases of a recipient complaining, we returned the money immediately, with an apology. The value included in that $200 charge was and is still, I firmly believe, impossible to gain from any other commercial marketing source. In fact, the average charge for a publicity professional is in excess of $80 for a single hour's work, while ours was a basic $200 for a year's service. We are absolutely confident therefore that we have provided excellent value for our service.*

Since we began to meet growing demand, we have invested hundreds of thousands of dollars in developing websites that provide interest, education and marketing advice to thousands of small businesses. We are extremely proud of the fact that due to our perseverance and vision we have been able to bring marketing advice and direct recognition to thousands of small businesses around the world, at a fraction of the cost of having a marketing organization provide similar results.

We are also hugely proud of the fact that we have been able to donate, on behalf of Society members, many millions of dollars to charities, particularly children's charities. To our knowledge, no other entity or individual in Australia has ever donated such sums to charities, in a short period of five years.

The attack in the media against me and our business has caused endless stress and concern among our members and has resulted in our decision to close all websites, unfortunately taking away cost-effective marketing from all our members here and around the world and bringing to an end our ability to provide substantial aid to needy causes.

We are most disappointed that some sections of the media have sought to make us appear as being less than totally honest and above board. On behalf of our many thousands of small business members, we believe an apology is warranted from those organizations and the journalists in question.

Only if we are asked by our loyal members, will we re-activate our websites and continue to provide service. Our future will be decided by whether our members consider they receive value, not by those who have not benefited."

Social media was first to react. There, Clyde was told by those who better understood those things, a massive response not only from members but from the now-huge number of followers as the messages and stories became viral with 13.7m likes and comments. Talk-back radio went ballistic as small businesses rang in fury to support the ISOCC and its fellow Societies.

CHAPTER TWENTY-THREE:
The circuit breaker

The story ran in full in virtually every major media outlet, including, to their credit, the Herald.

And as happens so often when one newspaper gets an exclusive, other newspapers, radio and television stations that had found themselves unwilling to follow the Herald's lead, now had their own stories to report. They covered the extraordinary outcry of small businesses and in doing so regurgitated every aspect of the global phenomenon that Clyde had started with that one latte in Cassareep. The Herald phone lines crashed.

And the Herald's writing on the subject began to slow. The rest of the media ran with the new angle, a request from hundreds of thousands of people on social media to bring back their Societies.

Our membership (only the smallest number of whom Clyde had ever met except anonymously in a coffee lounge) had risen in anger.

The statement and the communication with members made what they call in the PR trade 'a story killer'. Clyde had explained the unembellished facts and killed the rumours.

The focus of the anger had shifted from the Societies to the damage that had been done to small business and then to the difficulties of running small businesses generally.

Thousands of owners wrote, emailed, Facebooked and in one instance, marched. There was little left to say in the news, except perhaps to answer the question: "Who is this Clyde West?"

Annie and Clyde sat and watched with huge interest. Emails were so prolific the system had shut down. Clyde had to ring Nigel once more, now on his game boat off Nukualofa, Tonga. He fixed the problem overnight and the emails flowed once more.

Ramesh and his team answered every one with a stock reply, under Clyde's name, so now the Societies had addressed the wider audience and, critically, their own members.

But something had to be done to bring it to a conclusion. Clyde picked up the phone and rang the producer of Sixty Minutes.

"I'm willing to give you an exclusive interview," he said, *"for a fee."*

"Gloves off?"

"Yes, every question answered honestly and openly. Full access, except to my family, provided you donate a fee of $200,000 to the Children's Cancer Foundation on behalf of the members of the Societies."

Clyde spent the best part of a week being interviewed. The crew flew to Mumbai and met Ramesh, and to Tonga to meet Nigel. Michelle and Peter refused to speak and Lesley similarly told them to go away. Gerry wanted to be interviewed but was not thought to be an integral part of the tale. He complained he was so angry, he considered having someone fire Clyde again.

Clyde gave Sixty Minutes everything. There was a very good story to tell and he got on very well with the journo who just happened to have been a cadet on the Herald when he was a journalist.

The results the following Sunday night were very pleasing if Clyde said so himself.

It can be a pretty daunting thing to find yourself being interviewed on a television show, especially Sixty Minutes, but it can be made easy if you follow a few rules. Clyde found himself applying all the training tips that he'd used to coach prime ministers, CEO's, and Olympians over the years. First, he would coach them; you forget the cameras, the lights, and the sound man. You only talk to the interviewer and nobody else. You chat one-to-one with the interviewer. Once you master that, the environment becomes less foreign and more comfortable.

Second, you never go into the interview cold. Just as he had advised his clients over the years, Clyde first asked the interviewer for a list of areas to be discussed and before the cameras rolled, he deliberately spent minutes building rapport with the journalist, chatting to him about his career and how he felt about all the travel. Then Clyde asked the journalist what his first question would be and once he had that, he planned his first answer to make sure it included the key statement he wanted to get across. That gave him a degree of control.

Third, he did not go into the interviews to answer questions unless he was able to do so with one of his planned statements. Clyde addressed each question, but he made sure that in every answer he transitioned to another of his key statements.

He gave all the credit to others, to the lounge owners and retailers, to his team and to the web itself. Every statement stressed one of the same four themes: 1. Small business people are the backbone of every nation and they need help. 2. The objective was always to help small businesses everywhere. 3. The Recognition

Program was able to help them in the most cost-effective way possible and 4. It had given millions to charity.

Clyde emailed some seven hundred coffee lounge, pub, health food, restaurants, and bakers, to ring and email the producer and reporter in a coordinated bombardment, all offering to speak on his behalf. He gave the producer the names of 50 small businesses that had gone on to build quite substantial businesses as a result of being motivated by the ISOCC efforts. Twelve charities rang to say how valuable the donations had been and the positive change that occurred.

Case studies make strong evidence. That's letting your friends do the fighting!

It all went very well. Sixty Minutes told the incredible story of how a humble, retired coffee lover (that's me, said Clyde) had created a unique multi-million-dollar business by helping small businesses. And had then given much of the profit to charity. The fact that the ISOCC had issued certificates before the technical formation of the first Society was forgotten. The program visited the back-street call center in Mumbai and interviewed Ramesh, standing before some 600 young people who owed their livelihoods to the ISOCC and all the other Societies since started.

When the reporter asked to film Clyde addressing Ramesh's team, he once again practised what he had taught for years. He made sure that he ignored the cameras. He delivered complete thoughts to individuals in the room and his eye contact included everyone. Most people make the mistake of trying to scan their eyes over the crowd as if they want to talk to everyone. It's a bad technique that results in them connecting with nobody. Politicians frequently make the error of talking to the TV camera lens, which makes them appear stilted and stiff. Clyde ignored the lens and connected with Ramesh's people as if each one was the most important person in the room - and to him they were.

The 15-minute piece ended by reporting that Mr. West would not be allowing any further interviews, ever. He asked that his privacy and that of his family be respected.

The Sixty Minutes program was widely reported for the next two news days and on the following Sunday, in more thoughtful features. But Clyde waited until Tuesday the following week to send an email to every member, globally.

'Dear Member,

I want to thank you personally for what you and your fellow members have done, in response to the media attacks mounted against your society.

Due to your wonderful support, the truth has prevailed and has been widely reported on Sixty Minutes and in the general media. Despite the initial damage done to our reputations, we now feel we have been vindicated. Many of your fellow members have asked us to restart the Society and to continue its work championing small businesses like yours. We feel that we should do so. With your on-going support, we will undertake to continue to service your needs and provide a world-class marketing consultancy to assist you and other small businesses in your highly competitive battle to support your families and staff.

As always, the cost to you will be kept at a minimal level and all profits from this point will go to charity.'

He made a note to check if that would result in all memberships being tax-deductible, then he scribbled it out. *Enough!* he thought.

Ramesh sent the email to every member, of all 58 societies.

It was time for the final act.

Clyde rang Nigel and he called his general manager who uploaded each of the 58 sites again. Ten hours later, Nigel had every Society and every website going. Clyde was back in the business of recognition. And with a renewed interest in what the Recognition Program did.

EPILOGUE

Now, in a fairytale, the Societies would have kept growing, but they did not. A lot of the magic had gone. Everyone knew what the Societies were and how they started. There was no charisma attached to the names. There was a flurry of people joining up, more out of fun than anything, but each Society lost many of their members over the following few years.

Clyde transferred ownership to the General Manager running each Society and did so for the cost of the transfer. Most agreed to continue running the business for their not insignificant salaries and bonuses. Clyde didn't profit from the transfers, but he'd already made plenty and he told himself: *"the older you get, the lower your aspirations become."*

He also felt he'd reached the edge of his Recognition attention span. There was no challenge anymore. And there comes a time in every entrepreneur's life when the best thing you can do is to get out of the way and let better people take over.

* * *

Clyde West, two years later:

"I think a lot these days. Gerry and Martha come down from Budapest or Annie and I fly up. We occasionally meet in resorts around the world. I don't know how long that relationship will last because soon I'll stop paying Gerry his stipend. I may be a mate, but I'll never forget that he not only fired me but had a lackey do it for him.

"We go fishing with Nigel in his 70ft Riviera.

I still drink The Hunter Vineyard Gewurztraminers and Cabernet Sauvignon (www.thehuntervineyard.com.au) because, well we may have sold the vineyard, but we have a few bottles left. Annie still likes her Peroni. We watch the sun go down and we spend a deal of time walking through malls and shopping centres, looking for certificates and chatting with owners. One day we'll go back to Speightstown even though Cassareep no longer exists. Sam is now running a booming restaurant in Holetown, called Lemongrass.

I kept a copy of the mailing lists having appreciated at last the value of a database. So here's the concept: What if I sent another email to every single certificate holder around the world, saying they had been chosen to win a certificate? Not for coffee or baking, meat, booze, or any product, but for recognition of the one thing that above all makes them a success?

"What if we created The International Society for Exceptional Customer Service? What small businessperson wouldn't pay $200 for an 'International Exceptional Service Award', (color, ready for framing to suit your decor)?

Given inflation, perhaps they'd pay $250? I'd written a training program for some 350,000 people in a supermarket chain once.

Peter could arrange the formation of the Society. Nigel could do the IT. Ramesh and Peter's 280 franchisees could sell it. We'd need a bank account, but Ivan, now a Regional Manager, would have one of his people set it up. We'd need a website, but that's easy. I'd fill it with tips on things like eye contact, smiling, and customer service quotes like: "It's hard for a customer to catch your eye, if you don't throw it" and "Never walk back to the kitchen without picking up as you go" and " Get every customer's name and use it every time you see them" and "Share a Smile."

Let's say we only sold half a million of these certificates at net $200 each. That would be $10 million. But we could sell 750,000… $15 million. It wouldn't take much time or effort.

"Annie, we need to talk! I'll have a Moet."

The end

AUTHOR'S NOTE: I did create and award a certificate to the Cassareep cafe in Speightstown, Barbados. And in the course of my PR career I was a part of most of the PR stunts mentioned above . The training tips, plus a lot more, are taught by the excellent partners and consultants at rogenSi.

And finally, I really, REALLY wished I had thought to start an International Society for Coffee Connoisseurs. **So I did, www.ISOCC.com.au_and yes, we have issued a few free certificates to coffee lounges and bars.**

I wonder where it might go...

Neil Flett

ABOUT THE AUTHOR

Neil Flett's 13-year newspaper career began as a cadet journalist on The Auckland Star in New Zealand. He became a reporter and then Editor of one of the city's suburban newspapers, The South Auckland Courier. He was a reporter on The Western Morning News and Evening Herald in Plymouth England, followed by The Ealing News in London, RADIO 3AW in Melbourne and The Sydney Morning Herald. Returning to Auckland to build a yacht, he was a feature writer and sub-editor on the weekend 8 0'Clock newspaper.

After sailing back to Sydney with wife Marcia, he began a 13-year career in publicity and promotions when he joined The Sun newspaper as Promotions Manager then set up his own Publicity Company, Neil Flett Promotions, specialising in Exhibitions. He changed the name to Publicity Consultants Australia and sold his company to BBD&O, taking equity in their PR company Holt Public Relations.

Selling out three years later he began his 'third' career, in management training and communications taking the Australian franchise for the Peter Rogen and Associates presentation skills training program. Rogen Australia grew into franchises in New Zealand and then Asia,

Canada, and The United States. In 1993 Neil bought out the founder of the company and continued to grow the business globally, taking on partners. Under the guidance of the partners the business grew to have offices in 14 cities around the world and was eventually sold to the American company Teletech.

In the course of his career, he worked on Olympic Host City bids and coached Prime Ministers, Premieres, Government Ministers, sports champions and community leaders.

After retiring, Neil and Marcia ran a vineyard in The Hunter Valley and now have a truffiere in the Southern Highlands. He remains Chairman of the rogenSi Soul Foundation, and is a director of the Starlight Childrens Foundation and a Councillor on The Australia Day Council of NSW.